GCSE Drama

An Inspector Calls

by J.B. Priestley

Shameless lies, guilty secrets and a family with more drama than the West End... there's plenty to get your head around in *An Inspector Calls*.

But never fear. This brilliant CGP book takes the mystery out of answering questions about the play in your GCSE Drama exam. It explains everything you need to know — design, performance, staging, the lot!

What's more, there are plenty of practice questions to test what you've learnt, and a whole section of exam advice to help you score top marks. It's Goole's number one suspect for exam success.

The Play Guide

CONTENTS

CONTENTS

Section Four — Staging and Design

Section Five — Close Analysis

Section Six — Exam Advice

The Characters in 'An Inspector Calls'
'An Inspector Calls' Cartoon

Published by CGP

Editors:
Izzy Bowen
Zoe Fenwick
Josh James
Holly Robinson

Contributors:
Charlotte Bleakley
Ruth Kidman

With thanks to Graham Fletcher and Matt Topping for the proofreading.
With thanks to Emily Smith for the copyright research.

Acknowledgements:

With thanks to Mark Douet for permission to use the image on the cover and the image on page 4.

With thanks to iStock.com for permission to use the image on page 3.

With thanks to Vishal Sharma and the Altrincham Garrick Playhouse for permission to use the images on pages 3, 4, 5, 12, 13, 22, 25, 26, 30, 32, 34, 42, 43, 45, 47, 50, 51, 55, 57, 58, 61, 62, 66 & 67.

With thanks to Getty Images for permission to use the images on pages 1, 6, 7, 9, 14 & 16.

With thanks to ArenaPAL for permission to use the images on pages 2, 22, 23, 29, 30, 35, 37, 38, 39, 60 & 68.

With thanks to Photostage for permission to use the images on pages 50 & 62.

With thanks to Rex Features for permission to use the images on pages 11, 14, 15, 17, 21, 53, 54, 69 & 71.

With thanks to Simon Gough Photography for permission to use the images on pages 33, 36, 40, 41, 44, 59 & 70.

Image on page 8: Vote Labour election poster, 1945 (colour litho), British School, (20th century) / Private Collection / Peter Newark Pictures / Bridgeman Images

Image on page 56: Hitler as a speaker 1934 (photo) / © SZ Photo / Scherl / Bridgeman Images

ISBN: 978 1 78294 964 0
Printed by Elanders Ltd, Newcastle upon Tyne.
Clipart from Corel®

Based on the classic CGP style created by Richard Parsons.

Introduction to 'An Inspector Calls'

'An Inspector Calls' was written by J.B. Priestley

See p. 14-15 for more on J.B. Priestley.

1) *An Inspector Calls* was written in <u>1945</u>, but it's <u>set</u> in Britain in <u>1912</u>.

2) It's a play by <u>J.B. Priestley</u>, a British <u>playwright</u> and <u>author</u>.

3) *An Inspector Calls* includes <u>tragic elements</u> — it deals with <u>serious themes</u>, <u>distressing events</u> and it <u>doesn't</u> have a happy ending.

4) The play also shares features with <u>morality plays</u>, <u>well-made plays</u> and <u>crime thrillers</u> (see p. 20-21 for more).

5) The play has <u>three acts</u> and there are <u>no scenes</u> within each act. <u>No time passes</u> between the <u>end</u> of <u>one act</u> and the <u>start</u> of the <u>next</u> — instead the action runs <u>continuously</u> to represent the course of <u>one evening</u>.

An Inspector Calls on Stage

Directors need to know the <u>key features</u> of the play before they produce it on <u>stage</u>. Aspects of the play such as its <u>context</u> and <u>genres</u> might influence how it is <u>performed</u> and <u>designed</u>.

It's a play about social responsibility

An Inspector Calls is about a <u>wealthy family</u> who are questioned by a police inspector about the death of a young woman. The play's <u>themes</u> focus on how people <u>behave</u> and the <u>consequences</u> of their actions:

1) **Social responsibility** — the <u>idea</u> that people in a <u>society</u> have a <u>duty</u> to look after <u>everyone else</u>.

2) **Social class** — how people from some social classes <u>treat</u> people from other social classes.

3) **Gender inequality** — how ideas about <u>gender</u> influence the way people are <u>expected</u> to act.

4) **Age** — how age affects people's <u>views of other people</u> and their <u>willingness to change</u>.

5) **Reputation** — how some people are more concerned with <u>outward appearances</u> than about doing what's <u>morally right</u>.

An Inspector Calls on Stage

<u>Directors</u> should consider the <u>themes</u> that they want to emphasise when making <u>production decisions</u>. For example, a director might highlight the theme of <u>social class</u> (see p. 10-11) by having stagehands dressed in <u>rags</u> carry the set furniture onto the stage when the curtain first rises. This could <u>symbolise</u> how the Birlings have become <u>wealthy</u> at the expense of the <u>less fortunate</u>.

The play reflected British society at the time

1) The <u>events</u> of the play are entirely <u>made up</u>, but Priestley uses the <u>context</u> and <u>setting</u> of the play to comment on <u>real social issues</u> that existed in <u>British society</u> in the 1910s and 1940s.

- There was a wide <u>class divide</u> in Britain in 1912. The <u>upper and middle classes</u> controlled most of the <u>wealth</u> and <u>power</u>, and lots of them didn't really care about the <u>difficulties</u> faced by the <u>working classes</u>.

- When the play was <u>written</u> and <u>performed</u> in the <u>1940s</u>, Britain had been through the First and Second World Wars. Although the wars had caused some <u>changes</u> in British society (see p. 8-9), a <u>class divide</u> still existed.

© Jimmy Sime / Stringer / Getty Images

2) The Birling family live in a <u>fictional</u> town called Brumley, but Brumley could represent <u>any industrial town</u> in Britain in the 1910s. Priestley wanted the audience to <u>recognise</u> this setting, as well as the issues around <u>social class</u> in the play, so that they would apply the <u>messages</u> of the play to their <u>own lives</u>.

3) In particular, he wanted to <u>encourage</u> the audience to be more <u>considerate</u> of other members of society.

Introduction to 'An Inspector Calls'

'An Inspector Calls' is still relevant today

The themes and messages explored in the play are still relevant to modern audiences:

- Priestley's message about the importance of social responsibility is just as valid today — lots of people still believe that more should be done to help the less fortunate.
- The play explores social issues that exist in today's society — many people still face prejudice because of their gender or class.
- *An Inspector Calls* explores ideas about reputation and a person's willingness to change. These themes are universal — they are recognisable in any era and any society.

Effect on the Audience

These links mean *An Inspector Calls* is relatable — audiences are able to compare their own experiences to those faced by Priestley's characters, which makes it easier for them to engage with the play's messages.

Its dramatic features appeal to audiences

1) *An Inspector Calls* is one of Priestley's most famous plays, and its dramatic features and universal themes have contributed to its enduring success.

2) The play is entirely focused on the Birlings' and Gerald's involvement in Eva/Daisy's death — there aren't any subplots with different storylines to distract the audience from the main action.

3) There are plenty of revelations which maintain a tense atmosphere.

4) The single location (the Birlings' dining room) and the way that Priestley has the plot run continuously between the three acts help to maintain the pace and keep the audience engaged.

5) The shocking twist at the end of the play leaves the audience with lots of questions. Ending the play with a cliffhanger means the audience keeps thinking about the play long after it's finished.

See Section Two for more on the play's dramatic features and the techniques that Priestley uses.

There have been many adaptations

1) *An Inspector Calls* was first performed in St Petersburg in 1945 (see p. 16). It was later performed in London in 1946, and in New York in 1947.

2) Since then, there have been numerous theatrical productions. One of the most famous is a non-naturalistic version of the play directed by Stephen Daldry which originally opened in 1992 (see p. 17).

3) Daldry set the action in 1912 and 1940s wartime Britain. He used a split stage so that the two locations could be shown at the same time.

4) A film version of the play was released in 1954, and a made-for-TV movie was shown on the BBC in 2015. Although Eva/Daisy doesn't appear in the play, both film versions show her in flashbacks.

5) *An Inspector Calls* has also been adapted into a radio play several times — the pace of the dialogue and the way the plot unfolds means that it's well suited to a radio format. A version of the play was aired on BBC Radio 4 in 2010.

Eric and Sheila from the 1946 performance.

You won't have to write about adaptations in your exam, but it's useful to see how the play has been presented in different ways — directors often use other works for inspiration.

Who's Who in 'An Inspector Calls'

Arthur Birling...

... is a successful businessman who is well respected in Brumley. He owns a factory and is head of the Birling family.

Sybil Birling...

... is Arthur's wife. She's obsessed with manners and her status in society.

Eric Birling...

... is the Birlings' son and he's a heavy drinker. He's going to inherit his father's business.

Sheila Birling...

... is the Birlings' daughter. She's in her early twenties, and is engaged to Gerald.

Gerald Croft...

... is an upper-class businessman. He's about thirty, and is engaged to Sheila.

The Inspector...

... is a mysterious man who claims to be a police inspector. He's investigating the death of Eva Smith.

Edna...

... is the Birlings' parlourmaid. She doesn't have many lines, but she welcomes the Inspector into the house. She's usually the only working-class woman on stage.

Eva Smith/Daisy Renton...

... is the victim of the play. Most productions don't show her on stage. She might be lots of different girls. She might not even be dead...

Introduction

Plot Summary

'An Inspector Calls'... what happens when?

Here's a little recap of the main events of *An Inspector Calls*. It's a good idea to learn what happens when so that you know exactly how the plot progresses and how all the important events fit together.

Act One — one spring evening in 1912...

© Vishal Sharma/Altrincham Garrick Playhouse

- The Birling family are celebrating Sheila's engagement to Gerald. It all seems to be going well, but Sheila suspects that Gerald lost interest in her last summer.

- Arthur gives a speech to Eric and Gerald about business. He says that every man should look after himself.

- Inspector Goole arrives and says that a woman called Eva Smith has committed suicide by drinking disinfectant. He starts to question the family members, one by one.

- It turns out Arthur Birling sacked Eva Smith from his factory because she helped to lead a strike in protest against low wages. When Eva/Daisy got a new job at Milwards department store, Sheila asked for Eva/Daisy to be sacked because Sheila was jealous of her.

- The Inspector explains that Eva Smith then changed her name to Daisy Renton. Gerald appears shocked and Eric leaves.

Act Two — everyone's tangled up in the Inspector's investigation

- Although he wants to keep it a secret, Gerald eventually describes how he spent last summer with Daisy Renton — she was his mistress.

- Gerald is upset. Sheila returns his ring and Gerald leaves.

- The Inspector gets Sybil to confess that she persuaded the Women's Charity Organisation to reject Eva/Daisy's appeal for help. Eva/Daisy was pregnant at the time.

© Vishal Sharma/Altrincham Garrick Playhouse

- Sybil blames the father of Eva/Daisy's child for her death.

- Sheila guesses that the father of the child is Eric.

Plot Summary

Act Three — Eric brings shame to the family

- Eric returns. He knows that the Inspector has led everyone to the conclusion that he's the father of Eva/Daisy's unborn child.

© Vishal Sharma/Altrincham Garrick Playhouse

- He describes how he met Eva/Daisy at a bar, and drunkenly forced her to have sex. He got her pregnant and then stole money from his father's business to support her.

- When Eva/Daisy found out that the money was stolen, she refused to take any more, and turned to Sybil's charity for help. Eric says Sybil murdered her own grandchild by refusing to give her charity.

- The Inspector reminds the Birlings that we are all responsible for each other. He warns that unless everyone learns to look after each other, the lesson will have to be learnt later with greater suffering. He then leaves the house, and the Birlings are left to discuss the evening's events.

Act Three — the final twist...

- Gerald returns, having spoken to a police officer who doesn't recognise the name 'Goole'. Birling calls the police station to confirm there is no inspector called 'Goole' in the area.

© Vishal Sharma/Altrincham Garrick Playhouse

- Gerald calls the hospital and finds out that no one has committed suicide. Birling, Sybil and Gerald decide it's all been a hoax and start to relax.

- Sheila and Eric argue that they are all still guilty of treating someone badly.

- The phone rings. A young woman has just been found dead after drinking disinfectant, and the police are sending an inspector to question the Birling family...

Ring, ring — this is your future self calling...

... to say thanks for starting off your revision so well. Once you're confident you know what happens when in *An Inspector Calls*, reward yourself with a gold star, and move on to Section One — a handy section about the play's context and themes. If you're still hazy on the plot, or just want a break, flick to the cartoon at the back of the book.

Introduction

Britain in 1912

An Inspector Calls is set over 100 years ago — a time when the word "squiffy" was considered rude.

The play takes place over the course of one evening in 1912

1) *An Inspector Calls* is set in <u>Britain</u> in <u>spring 1912</u> — two years before the outbreak of <u>World War One</u>.

2) The <u>pre-war period</u> was a time of <u>prosperity</u> for the upper and middle classes, whereas the working class were <u>struggling</u> to make ends meet (see p. 7).

3) The <u>inequality</u> in the <u>class system</u> was very pronounced at this time, which made it <u>easier</u> for Priestley to point out its <u>flaws</u>.

4) Although the events of the play are <u>fictional</u>, the dialogue refers to <u>real-life</u> events, like the sailing of the *Titanic* and the <u>miners' strike</u> (see p. 7).

© Photo 12 / Universal Images Group/ Getty Images

Miners' strike 1912.

Effect on the Audience

Referring to real <u>historical</u> events makes the setting and context <u>clearer</u> for the audience, as well as making the world of the play more <u>believable</u>.

***An Inspector Calls* on Stage**

The context of the play will affect choices about <u>costume</u> and <u>set design</u>. In a <u>naturalistic production</u> (see p. 22), designers might take inspiration from the <u>fashions</u> and <u>styles</u> of <u>1912</u> to make the set and costumes more <u>authentic</u>.

The play is set in Brumley — a fictional town in the Midlands

1) The Birlings live in Brumley, where Mr Birling owns a <u>factory</u>. Brumley is described as "an <u>industrial</u> city in the <u>North Midlands</u>".

2) Although the town is <u>fictional</u>, it's <u>based on real</u> industrial towns of the era. In 1912, cities like this would have had <u>factories</u> and thousands of terraced houses for all the <u>factory workers</u>.

3) Here are the <u>key locations</u> in the play:

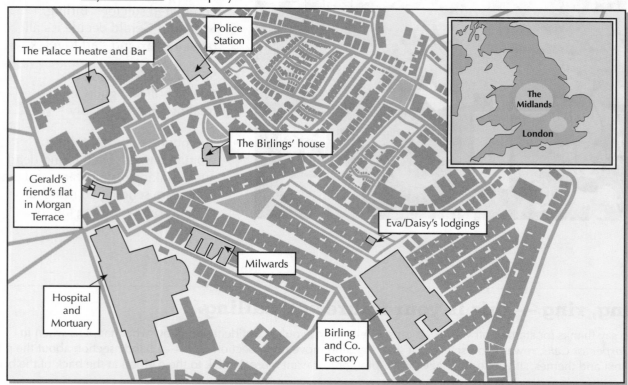

Britain in 1912

Britain was a very different place in 1912

There's more on social class on p. 10-11, and gender and family life on p. 12-13.

1) In the early 20th century, British society was <u>divided</u> into three <u>classes</u> — the <u>upper class</u>, the <u>middle class</u> and the <u>working class</u>. The upper and middle classes had most of the <u>money</u> and most of the <u>power</u>.

2) Only <u>men</u> who owned <u>property</u> could vote — this meant that working-class people often <u>didn't</u> have a voice. <u>Women</u> weren't allowed to <u>vote</u> in elections <u>at all</u>.

3) Women were expected to <u>marry</u>, have <u>children</u> and <u>obey</u> their husbands.

4) A <u>boom</u> in <u>industry</u> during the 19th century meant there was demand for <u>cheap labour</u> in <u>factories</u> and industries like <u>mining and shipbuilding</u>. Many people left <u>rural areas</u> for the promise of <u>work</u> in the cities.

5) Often, these jobs were <u>dangerous</u> and <u>difficult</u> with <u>long hours</u>. The <u>low wages</u> and the <u>poor living conditions</u> meant that lots of working-class people lived in <u>poverty</u> and had <u>short life expectancies</u>.

6) However, things were starting to <u>change</u>. In 1900, the <u>Labour party</u> was formed to represent the interests of the working class, and in 1912, over a <u>million</u> workers across Britain campaigned for <u>fairer wages</u> for miners — this was known as the National Miners' Strike. It was the <u>largest strike</u> in Britain at the time, and it showed that the working class was starting to <u>fight back</u> against the upper and middle classes.

© Topical Press Agency / Stringer/ Getty Images

A couple in a slum dwelling, 1912.

Context

This <u>historical context</u> is reflected in the play. When Eva worked at Mr Birling's factory, she asked him for <u>fairer wages</u>. When he <u>refused</u>, she helped to organise a <u>strike</u> and he <u>fired</u> her.

There was little help for people in need

1) During the 19th century, the upper and middle classes <u>categorised</u> people living in <u>poverty</u> as either '<u>deserving</u>' or '<u>undeserving</u>' of help. The 'deserving poor' were people who were seen to have fallen on <u>hard times</u> through <u>no fault of their own</u>, perhaps through <u>illness</u> or <u>old age</u>.

2) The 'undeserving poor' were people who, in the eyes of the wealthy, faced hardship because of their <u>own bad choices</u>, e.g. <u>laziness</u> or <u>drunkenness</u>.

3) This idea of the deserving and undeserving poor caused a <u>dilemma</u> for the wealthy — they wanted to help the 'deserving poor' <u>without encouraging</u> qualities of <u>idleness</u> and <u>recklessness</u> in the 'undeserving poor'.

4) <u>Charities</u> were set up for people who were thought to really <u>deserve</u> help.

5) It was quite common for charities to <u>interview</u> the people who came to them for help — a panel would then decide whether the applicant <u>deserved</u> the help they were asking for. In the play, Sybil Birling sits on the <u>board</u> for one of these charities. She convinces the committee to <u>refuse</u> Eva/Daisy's request for help.

Social Responsibility

- The idea of <u>social responsibility</u> was <u>uncommon</u> in 1912.

- Mr and Mrs Birling think Eva/Daisy is to <u>blame</u> for her problems — Sybil <u>turns Eva/Daisy away</u> from her charity because she <u>doesn't believe</u> her story and thinks the father should be <u>made responsible</u>.

- Priestley <u>challenges</u> this view by showing how Eva/Daisy was the <u>victim</u> of <u>other people's behaviour</u>.

EXAM TIP

This Drama GCSE could cause a national minors' strike...

The context of the play is important — Priestley wanted to comment on people's attitudes to each other. Think about how you could represent this context to get his message across if you were staging the play.

Britain in 1945

Although the play is set in 1912, Priestley wrote it in 1945 — this time period is really important too.

There were many significant events between 1912 and 1945

1914-1918 — World War One. Over 700,000 British soldiers are killed in action.

1928 — All men and women over the age of 21 are now allowed to vote. Working-class men and women have more power to shape the government.

1930s — The Great Depression. The Great Depression was a global economic slump. There was widespread unemployment and poverty which affected both the middle and working classes.

1939-1945 — World War Two. Approximately 384,000 British soldiers are killed in action, and 376,000 are wounded. A further 67,000 civilians are killed as a result of military action, e.g. bombing.

World War Two had a huge impact on British society

1) The war affected all aspects of British life, not only while it was happening, but after it had ended too.

2) Millions of people from all three classes fought during the war — lots of upper, middle and working-class soldiers had to live, work and fight together. This made some people question the fairness of Britain's social structure. Movements like socialism, which called for social change, became more popular.

3) Many women who had not worked before had to take over men's jobs during the war. They were reluctant to give up employment once the war ended. This helped to change attitudes towards women, and caused people to start questioning gender roles.

> Socialism is a set of beliefs calling for the more equal sharing of wealth and power.

4) World War Two caused massive devastation — towns and cities were destroyed by bombing and most families lost loved ones. After the war, some people vowed that this should never happen again and wanted to work together to build a better society.

In 1945 there was a desire for social change

1) In July 1945, the UK held the first general election since before the war began. The Labour party won by a landslide, defeating the Conservative party and the popular wartime Prime Minister, Winston Churchill.

2) The recent memory of the war had a big influence on the election results. The Labour party promised to focus on social reform and the creation of a welfare state. They wanted to create a 'cradle to grave' system where members of society had access to help and support throughout their entire lives. This was particularly important after the war, as many former soldiers returned home in need of employment and medical care.

3) Labour's victory marked a change in British attitudes — more voters supported the idea of helping the ill, poor and vulnerable compared to before the war.

4) *An Inspector Calls* was written just before the Labour party came to power, but the ideas in the play reflect the desire for change that was felt by many in the run up to the election.

A Labour poster from 1945.

Section One — Context and Themes

Britain in 1945

Priestley used a post-war perspective to look back on the past

1) Setting the play in 1912 allowed Priestley to <u>reflect</u> on the events that happened between <u>1912 and 1945</u>.

2) The class system in 1945 was <u>less defined</u> than in 1912, but <u>class divisions</u> still <u>existed</u>. Priestley wanted to remind audiences in 1945 <u>how far things had come</u>, but he also wanted to warn them about the dangers of the class system and <u>prevent</u> society from going back to the way things were in 1912.

3) Priestley wanted to use his play to <u>encourage social reform</u>. <u>Post-war audiences</u> were likely to feel <u>optimistic</u> about the future, thanks in part to the <u>social changes</u> that had come about as a result of the wars. This meant they were more likely to <u>agree</u> with the Inspector's message.

4) The Inspector suggests that if the Birlings (and society) <u>don't</u> learn to take <u>responsibility for others</u>, then they will be taught to change through "<u>fire and blood and anguish</u>". This threat would have reminded audiences in 1945 of the <u>World Wars</u>. Implying that the World Wars were a <u>consequence</u> of selfish behaviour would have encouraged audiences to <u>change</u> their ways.

© Hulton Deutsch/ Corbis Historical/ Getty Images

Flowers laid on a soldier's grave, 1944.

A modern-day audience might receive the play differently

<u>Changes</u> in <u>attitudes</u>, e.g. towards class or gender, and the availability of <u>social welfare</u> such as the NHS and jobseeker's allowance, mean that audiences today might <u>react differently</u> to the play than 1940s audiences.

Audiences in the 1940s may have been <u>shocked</u> by Eva/Daisy's actions. <u>Sexual relationships</u> outside of marriage were <u>strongly disapproved of</u>, and <u>pregnant</u>, <u>unmarried women</u> were often <u>judged</u> by society.	A <u>modern audience</u> would probably find Mrs Birling's treatment of Eva/Daisy more shocking than the thought of Eva/Daisy being an <u>unmarried single mother</u>.
1940s audiences might have been quite <u>uncomfortable</u> with Sheila's behaviour — she <u>interrupts</u> and <u>challenges</u> the male characters. Even in the 1940s, women were expected to <u>respect</u> men's opinions.	Women have more <u>freedom</u> in today's society, so an audience would react more <u>positively</u> to Sheila's <u>defiant</u> behaviour.
1940s audiences were used to living in a society where there <u>wasn't much</u> government help available for those who needed it. This would have made them more <u>aware</u> of the importance of <u>social responsibility</u>.	Most modern audience members would have <u>grown up</u> with <u>government-funded social welfare</u>. They might take these things <u>for granted</u> and not understand the <u>significance</u> of the Inspector's message.

REVISION TASK

Crikey, this was an eventful time period...

Imagine you are directing a performance of 'An Inspector Calls'. Write a paragraph about how you would make the play's messages relevant to a modern audience. Remember to include:

1) How social attitudes have changed since 1945.
2) Which of the play's messages could be relevant today.
3) How you would use your position as director to send these messages to the audience.

Tick list:
✓ social and historical context
✓ play's messages
✓ audience response

Social Class

Most people in 1912 were categorised as 'haves' or 'have-nots' — those with money and those without.
I categorise people as 'haves' and 'have-nots' too — those who have read this page, and those who have not.

There was a clear class structure in the early 20th century

Several things contributed to what class you were in, but it mainly came down to money
— those who had it, and those who didn't. There were three main classes:

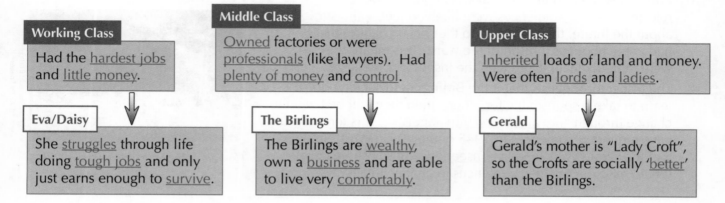

Working Class

Had the hardest jobs and little money.

Eva/Daisy

She struggles through life doing tough jobs and only just earns enough to survive.

Middle Class

Owned factories or were professionals (like lawyers). Had plenty of money and control.

The Birlings

The Birlings are wealthy, own a business and are able to live very comfortably.

Upper Class

Inherited loads of land and money. Were often lords and ladies.

Gerald

Gerald's mother is "Lady Croft", so the Crofts are socially 'better' than the Birlings.

Social class had a big impact on people's lives

> Eva/Daisy and Sheila are quite close in age, but their lives are very different because of their social class.

Social class affected almost every aspect of a person's life:

1) **Education and occupation**: Most working-class people left education at a young age to take up low-skilled, low-paying jobs to support their family. Middle-class men would stay in education and take higher-paying jobs, while upper-class men might not need to work due to their family's money. Upper and middle-class women were not expected to work.

> As a working-class woman, Eva/Daisy needs a job to support herself. She has low-skilled jobs as a factory worker and a shop assistant. Sheila is a middle-class woman — her family support her, so she doesn't need to work.

2) **Clothing**: Working-class people had little money, so often had very few items of clothing. What they had was typically second-hand or re-used from old, worn pieces of clothing. Members of the middle and upper classes had bigger disposable incomes, so were able to spend more on clothes.

> Sheila has an "account" at Milwards which is described as a "good shop" that sells "pretty clothes" — she can afford to spend money on her appearance.

3) **Speech**: Members of the working class usually spoke in a stronger local accent and used more dialect words than members of the higher classes. Members of the upper classes were more likely to use Standard English and Received Pronunciation.

> Mr Birling is said to be "*rather provincial in his speech*". This suggests he might have a regional accent, implying that he is from a lower social class than his wife and Gerald.

4) **Nutrition**: Many of the working classes lived in poverty, so they often didn't have enough to eat. The middle and upper classes would be more likely to have lavish dinners which consisted of several courses.

> In Act One, the Birlings and Gerald have just enjoyed a "*good dinner*" and they can afford luxuries like port. Gerald buys Eva/Daisy food because she's "actually hungry".

Section One — Context and Themes

Social Class

Working-class people were ignored or badly treated

1) Upper and middle-class people were often <u>prejudiced</u> towards the working class — they thought working-class people were <u>lazy</u> and <u>immoral</u>, and didn't deserve the same <u>rights</u> as they did.

2) As a result, working-class people were often <u>discriminated against</u> or <u>ignored</u>, rather than <u>helped</u>.

3) Priestley portrays the Birling family as having a <u>limited</u> sense of <u>social responsibility</u> for the less well-off.

- Mr Birling <u>refuses</u> to pay Eva/Daisy <u>more money</u> when she asks for fairer wages. He doesn't <u>care</u> that he's paying her <u>very little</u> — he's only bothered about making <u>more money</u> for himself.
- Sheila gets Eva/Daisy <u>fired</u> because she is jealous — she <u>doesn't care</u> about how this affects Eva/Daisy.
- Mrs Birling is <u>prejudiced</u> against Eva/Daisy — she doesn't think that Eva/Daisy would turn down <u>stolen money</u> ("As if a girl of that sort would ever refuse money!").
- Mr and Mrs Birling don't feel <u>remorse</u> for Eva/Daisy's death — their <u>concern</u> is for their reputations.

Reputation

A person's reputation was <u>important</u> to the upper and middle classes because it could affect their chances in <u>society</u> and <u>business</u>. Mr and Mrs Birling are desperate to be seen as <u>upstanding</u> members of society because they don't want to jeopardise Mr Birling's chances of receiving a <u>knighthood</u>. Meanwhile, Eva/Daisy's reputation as a member of the working class causes others to <u>treat her badly</u>.

Priestley uses the play to comment on social class

1) Priestley uses the play to criticise the class system and <u>reveal</u> its <u>unfairness</u> — he uses the Birlings as <u>caricatures</u> of all the <u>bad qualities</u> he thought the middle and upper classes had.

2) Because the Birlings are presented as <u>unflattering, middle-class stereotypes</u>, the audience quickly recognises that they are mostly <u>flawed, unsympathetic characters</u>. This makes the audience feel more <u>empathy</u> for Eva/Daisy and helps them <u>understand</u> the Inspector's message.

3) The play isn't just about <u>one family's scandal</u> — it shows how Priestley saw <u>society</u>. Priestley suggests that the Birlings' arrogant and selfish behaviour is <u>common</u> to the middle and upper classes.

4) Priestley presents the working class as <u>victims</u> of the <u>class system</u> — although Eva/Daisy is a fictional <u>character</u>, the miseries she suffered were probably quite <u>realistic</u>. The fact that it's unclear whether she was <u>one person</u> or <u>several people</u> highlights how <u>common</u> it was for the working classes to be <u>treated badly</u> by those in positions of power.

The Inspector is classless

1) The Inspector doesn't seem to belong to a <u>social class</u>. He's not a part of the Birlings' <u>middle-class world</u> — he <u>doesn't play golf</u> and he's <u>not impressed</u> by Mr Birling's social connections. He doesn't belong to the working class either — as an inspector, he's a <u>middle-ranking</u> police officer.

2) He doesn't follow the <u>social rules</u> of the period— he <u>interrupts</u> the other characters, speaks "<u>savagely</u>" and doesn't care if he <u>offends</u> anyone. The idea of treating someone more <u>politely</u> due to their higher class is <u>irrelevant</u> to him.

3) This <u>isolation</u> from the class system allows the Inspector to <u>criticise</u> the way that the classes <u>behave</u>.

© Alastair Muir/REX/Shutterstock

EXAM TIP

I didn't do my homework because class shouldn't matter...

Think about how a director could show the classless nature of the Inspector on stage. It could be shown through his costume, his physical performance or the manner in which he speaks to the other characters.

Gender Roles, Age and Family Structure

Gender roles: not as fun as forward rolls or bacon rolls — but more likely to come up in the exam.

Gender roles were fixed in 1912

1) In the early 20th century, men and women had different roles in society and in the family.

2) Men were often the breadwinners — they earned the money to provide for their families. Most high-status jobs in society were occupied by middle-class men. Working-class men often worked in low-skilled, manual jobs.

There's more about social class on p. 10-11.

3) Middle and upper-class women would stay at home to look after the house and family. Working-class women would usually have to work as well as looking after the house and children, but they were often paid a lot less then men.

4) There was a typical family structure in 1912 — the father was seen as the head of the family, and his wife and children were expected to respect him.

5) Children were expected to obey their parents and they would usually marry someone their family approved of, often so they could improve the family's social and financial position.

6) Sons were often expected to take over the family business.

7) The Birlings represent a typical middle-class family:

Reputation

People were expected to marry someone from a similar class. Eric and Gerald's relationships with Eva/Daisy would have caused a scandal because she was working class, so they both keep their relationship with her a secret.

- Arthur is the breadwinner — he supports his wife and children. Sheila and Sybil don't work.

- Arthur acts as the head of the family. His monologues in Act One show how he expects the rest of the family to listen to, and agree with, his views.

- Mr and Mrs Birling are happy that Sheila is marrying Gerald — Gerald's family is socially superior to the Birlings, and Gerald's father runs a rival business to Arthur's. Arthur hopes that the marriage will improve the family's social status and his business prospects.

- Arthur gives Eric and Gerald business advice in Act One. He expects that they will carry on the family businesses.

The Birlings and Gerald reflect gender stereotypes

1) In 1912, men and women were expected to behave in a certain way, and were presumed to have certain characteristics.

2) At the start of *An Inspector Calls*, the Birlings and Gerald seem to conform to these middle and upper-class gender stereotypes.

© Vishal Sharma/Altrincham Garrick Playhouse

- The men are interested in current affairs and business — Arthur talks about the miners' strike and Eric asks about the possibility of war. Sybil tells Sheila to expect that Gerald will be preoccupied with work when they are married.

- The women, however, are presented as shallow and interested in trivial, material things — Sheila admires her engagement ring, and Eric says that women are "potty" about clothes.

- The men try to protect the women from the Inspector's questions — Mr Birling thinks that Sheila is too sensitive to hear the gruesome details of Eva/Daisy's death.

Character — The Inspector

The Inspector doesn't conform to stereotypes. He doesn't try to protect Sheila and Sybil from Eva/Daisy's death. He treats everyone the same.

Gender Roles, Age and Family Structure

Sheila challenges some stereotypes

1) As the play progresses, Sheila changes — she rebels against the family structure and gender stereotypes.

2) She doesn't want to be protected from the Inspector's questions — she refuses to leave the room at the start of Act Two and she wants to hear about Gerald's affair.

3) She doesn't know whether she'll marry Gerald or not at the end of the play — she needs time to decide for herself rather than just following her father's wishes.

4) She shows less respect to her parents — she calls them "childish". This suggests that Mr and Mrs Birling no longer have authority over her.

5) By the end of the play, Sheila has evolved as a character. She makes up her own mind about the Inspector's message and refuses to let Gerald or her parents tell her what to think.

Effect on the Audience

The Inspector points out the hypocrisy of the men's attitudes to women — they want to protect Sheila from "unpleasant and disturbing things", but don't care about the unpleasant things they put Eva/Daisy through. This emphasises how working-class people were discriminated against by the middle and upper classes.

Character — Eric

Sheila isn't the only character who rebels against the family structure — Eric is "shouting" at Mr Birling by the end of the play. This suggests that Eric no longer respects his father.

Staging

A set designer could use levels to show how Sheila has changed. Using a rostrum to raise her above Gerald and her parents could suggest how she has become morally superior to them.

The characters' reactions show their differences in age

1) The different ways the Birlings and Gerald react to the Inspector's revelations reflect their different ages — the characters represent the attitudes of the different generations in society in general.

2) When they are questioned by the Inspector, Mr and Mrs Birling won't accept any responsibility for their role in Eva/Daisy's death.

3) The younger generation are different — Sheila and Eric show remorse. Through them, Priestley suggests that there's a chance for a more equal and fairer society in the future.

4) Although he's a younger character, Gerald's views are similar to Mr and Mrs Birling's and he doesn't seem to have learned from the Inspector's visit, telling Sheila at the end "Everything's all right now".

© Vishal Sharma/Altrincham Garrick Playhouse

Social Class

The fact that Gerald is of the younger generation but remains unchanged suggests that a more caring future isn't inevitable — people can choose whether to change or not. Priestley is also criticising the upper classes by suggesting that they're more set in their ways and less likely to change.

EXAM TIP

And I thought my family was complicated...

When writing about how an actor might portray a character, think carefully about how they could use physical and vocal skills to show how the character's relationships with the other family members change.

J.B. Priestley

J.B. Priestley's name might be new to you, but he was pretty famous in his day — he was a popular writer and made a series of inspiring wartime radio shows. Priestley's views on society can be seen throughout his work.

J.B. Priestley was a British playwright

1) J.B. Priestley was born in Bradford, a city in West Yorkshire, in 1894. He died in 1984 aged 89.

2) His parents were from poor backgrounds, but his own upbringing was comfortable.

3) He started his successful writing career by writing articles for newspapers, and also published novels before he began writing plays in the 1930s. *An Inspector Calls* is considered his most famous play.

4) His upbringing influenced his writing — several of his works are set in Yorkshire (*Time and the Conways*, *I Have Been Here Before* and *When We Are Married*).

5) Later in life, Priestley was awarded both a peerage (an invitation to become a member of the British nobility) and a knighthood, but he refused them both.

J.B. Priestley.

© Hulton Deutsch/ Corbis Historical/ Getty Images

When Priestley was growing up, people were fighting for change

1) Priestley wanted to be a writer from a young age. Instead of going to university, he left school at 16 to work as a clerk in a wool firm — he wanted to gain experience of the world that he could use for his writing.

2) At the wool firm, Priestley was exposed to the political opinions of the people he worked and socialised with, and this is probably where he began to develop socialist views (see p. 8).

3) Throughout Priestley's teenage years, demand for universal suffrage (all adults having the right to vote) was growing. Men and women campaigned for the vote so that their interests could be equally represented in government.

4) The women's suffrage movement in particular became increasingly militant and high-profile until the start of the First World War in 1914.

Emmeline Pankhurst, a prominent member of the suffragette movement, is arrested.

© Granger/REX/Shutterstock

He was influenced by the First World War

Priestley fought in the First World War (1914-1918) — he was wounded, but survived. His experiences had a profound effect on him:

- During the war, he witnessed first-hand how damaging class prejudice could be. The British army was forced to expand rapidly when the war began, and hundreds of new, inexperienced generals were appointed to lead regiments made up mostly of working-class infantry.

- The majority of these generals came from the middle and upper classes — many had family connections in the army and a university-level education. They were known as the 'officer class', and some people have blamed them for the loss of many working-class lives due to poor decisions. Priestley was very critical of the officer class in his memoirs.

- Some historians believe that Priestley suffered from 'survivor's guilt' after returning from the war — he wanted to make something of his life to justify having survived when many of his friends did not.

J.B. Priestley

Priestley expressed socialist views in his works

1) Priestley became <u>increasingly concerned</u> with how people were <u>treated</u> in society. He began to use his works to <u>criticise class inequality</u> and promote his ideas about <u>social responsibility</u>.

2) <u>Socialism</u> grew in popularity in the mid-20th century, and Priestley sympathised with the socialist belief that <u>wealth</u> and <u>power</u> should be <u>shared more equally</u> in society.

3) In 1934, he published *English Journey* — an account of his <u>travels</u> in England. Priestley used it to express his views on the <u>social problems</u> he witnessed during the Great Depression (see p. 8).

4) In <u>1940</u>, during the Second World War, Priestley began broadcasting a very popular <u>weekly radio programme</u> called *Postscripts*. The radio programme helped to boost public <u>morale</u> by <u>supporting</u> the troops and <u>praising</u> the British public's <u>determination and resilience</u>.

5) Priestley also used the programme to <u>comment</u> on policies from the right-wing, Conservative-led government that he <u>didn't agree with</u> and to promote his image of a <u>new social order</u> after the war based on the idea of <u>community</u>. His radio programme was eventually <u>cancelled</u> because it was seen to be too <u>left-wing</u> and <u>critical</u> of the government.

> Left-wing beliefs suggest the government should do more to support people in society, e.g. through a welfare state. Right-wing beliefs suggest the government should have a smaller role in people's lives.

Priestley uses the Inspector as a mouthpiece

1) Some people have suggested that Priestley uses the Inspector as a '<u>mouthpiece</u>' to express his views on <u>social class</u> and <u>inequality</u>.

2) The Inspector doesn't belong to the <u>class system</u> presented in the play (see p. 11) — he is an <u>outsider</u>. This gives him an <u>objective</u> viewpoint which gives <u>authority</u> to the things he says.

3) However the Inspector <u>doesn't</u> take a <u>neutral</u> position — he's on Eva/Daisy's <u>side</u>, and he <u>doesn't hesitate</u> to tell the Birlings what he thinks of them.

4) This is most clear during the Inspector's <u>final speech</u>. He's speaking to the <u>Birling family</u>, urging them to consider the effects of their actions on other people's lives, but the speech could also be directed at the <u>audience</u>.

© Alastair Muir/REX/Shutterstock

Character — The Inspector

A production could make the <u>connection</u> between the Inspector and Priestley <u>stronger</u>, e.g. by having the actor playing the Inspector use a <u>Yorkshire accent</u> or by dressing him in a <u>1940s-style suit</u>.

5) The Inspector is a bit like a <u>playwright</u> too — he seems to know <u>far more</u> than a normal police inspector would, and he uses <u>language</u> to get <u>reactions</u> from other people (see p. 24).

6) The Inspector also '<u>directs</u>' the action on stage, e.g. by showing the <u>photo</u> of Eva/Daisy to <u>one person at a time</u> to gradually reveal each family member's role in her death.

7) The play (and Priestley) has a <u>clear message</u> about <u>looking after</u> other people in society, and the Inspector is used to <u>deliver it</u>.

EXAM TIP

I prefer to use my harmonica as a mouthpiece...

Make sure that you understand how Priestley's life impacted his views and the work that he produced. This will help you pick out his intentions as a playwright and make choices about performing the play.

The Play on Stage

So, that's the background to the play done and dusted. Now for the real drama bit — how it's been staged over time. The way a play is performed can make a big difference to how it's interpreted by the audience.

Theatre was very popular in the 1940s

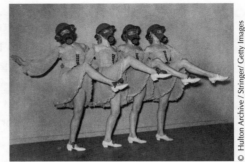

Theatre dancers practise with gas masks.

1) During the <u>Second World War</u>, a considerable amount of <u>funding</u> was given to <u>ballet, opera and drama</u> — this allowed theatre groups to go on <u>tour</u> and bring the arts to <u>remote rural areas</u>, as well as <u>industrial towns</u>.

2) This made theatre more <u>accessible</u> and allowed many people to experience it for the <u>first time</u>.

3) Going to the theatre was a way of <u>boosting</u> the public's <u>morale</u> by providing a <u>respite</u> from the <u>realities of wartime life</u>.

4) However, theatre had <u>another purpose</u>. Funding was mainly given to <u>serious</u> drama with an <u>educational value</u> — CEMA (the Council for Encouragement of Music and the Arts) wanted to showcase Britain's <u>cultural heritage</u> through <u>quality theatre</u>.

5) CEMA also wanted to promote <u>thought-provoking theatre</u> to show that Britain was an <u>enlightened</u> country, and to <u>distance</u> Britain from the <u>censorship</u> and <u>oppression</u> of Nazi Germany.

Plays were becoming more political

1) During the first half of the 20th century, society faced a lot of <u>upheaval</u>, including <u>two World Wars</u> and the <u>Great Depression</u> (see p. 8). Some dramatists were influenced by this <u>political climate</u>.

2) One such dramatist was <u>Bertolt Brecht</u> (1898-1956). Brecht <u>opposed fascism</u>, and he wrote several plays which <u>criticised</u> the Nazi regime, including *Fear and Misery of the Third Reich* (1938).

3) Brecht developed a style of theatre known as <u>Epic Theatre</u>, which uses techniques to <u>remind</u> the audience that they are watching a play. Distancing the audience from the story allows them to <u>focus</u> on the (usually <u>political</u>) message of a play.

Effect on the Audience
Although Priestley describes a <u>realistic</u> set in the stage directions for *An Inspector Calls*, he also <u>acknowledges</u> that a production could *"dispense with"* it. A director who wanted to <u>focus</u> the audience's attention on the <u>message</u> of the play may choose to incorporate elements of <u>Epic Theatre</u> into their production.

'An Inspector Calls' was first performed in Russia

1) When Priestley was ready to stage *An Inspector Calls* in 1945, all suitable British theatres were <u>booked</u>, so Priestley took the play to <u>Russia</u> (then known as the USSR) instead.

2) The play was <u>translated</u> into Russian. It was first performed in <u>St Petersburg</u> (then called Leningrad), titled *This You Will Not Forget*, and then in <u>Moscow</u>, titled *He Came*.

3) Priestley was invited to the opening in Russia and received <u>standing ovations</u> from audiences.

4) The play was very <u>well received</u>, possibly because of its <u>socialist ideas</u>. At the time, Russia was a <u>Communist</u> country under the rule of Stalin. Many of the ideas in *An Inspector Calls* about <u>class</u> and <u>wealth inequality</u> reflected feelings people had in Russia at the time.

> Communism is the idea that everything in society should be owned by the community, and everyone should contribute and receive equally.

The Play on Stage

The first British audiences weren't so keen on the play

1) *An Inspector Calls* opened in the UK on 1st October 1946 at London's New Theatre (now the Noël Coward Theatre). It was staged by the Old Vic theatre company, whose own theatre had been damaged by bombing during the Second World War.

2) The first British production used a naturalistic style. Afterwards, Priestley felt that this style wasn't particularly effective because audiences were more focused on the storyline rather than the play's message.

3) The play received mixed reviews from critics — many felt that the play's content was too serious, that there was too much talking and that the Birling family were tedious. However, others were more complimentary and particularly liked the twist at the end.

4) The difference in opinion may have been influenced by the backgrounds of the audience. Many audience members would have been from the upper and middle classes, and the play's critique of middle and upper-class life and values could have been interpreted as an attack on the audience.

5) As well as this, some audiences might have wanted to forget the atrocities of war and look to a brighter future. They wanted fantasy and escapism, not the lecture provided by the Inspector.

The play was revived using non-naturalistic elements

1) The play became less popular in the middle of the 20th century, possibly due to the rise of 'kitchen sink' dramas, which showed ordinary working-class life. Even though it has a socialist message, Priestley's play still mainly features middle and upper-class characters.

2) The play was revived in 1992 with a production by the National Theatre, directed by Stephen Daldry. The production used many non-naturalistic elements, including setting it in two different time periods and using a collapsing set (see p. 22).

3) The production was intended to criticise recent British politics. Britain had been under a Conservative government for thirteen years, led for most of that time by Margaret Thatcher. Thatcher was a divisive figure — although lots of people voted for her, many others were unhappy about her attitude to society and the working class. They felt that 'Thatcherism' promoted looking after yourself rather than helping others.

4) The 1992 production was very successful, perhaps because it felt so relevant to issues at the time. Daldry's production has continued to be popular, with several tours and many performances in the West End.

© Jane Hobson/REX/Shutterstock

Stephen Daldry's production.

REVISION TASK

This play is tough in English, let alone in Russian...

Imagine you are directing 'An Inspector Calls'. Write a list of pros and cons for using a naturalistic set versus a non-naturalistic one. Which do you think is more effective for getting across the play's message? Think about:

1) The different features of each style of set.
2) The effects of these features on the audience.
3) How a modern-day audience might react to the play.

Tick list:
✓ different set styles
✓ audience response
✓ modern perspective

Practice Questions

That's your first section done, and blimey, what a section it was. Here's the really fun part though — practice questions. Work through these quick questions to check how much information you've absorbed. When you've done that, answer the in-depth questions below — try to write about a paragraph for each of them.

Quick Questions

1) Give two examples of how Britain in 1912 was different to the present day.

2) What was the difference between the 'deserving' and 'undeserving' poor?

3) Give two examples of how World War Two changed British society.

4) Why might audiences in the 1940s have been particularly receptive to the Inspector's message?

5) Name a character from the play who belongs to the upper class.

6) Give one way in which Sheila conforms to gender stereotypes at the start of the play.

7) Briefly explain how the First World War influenced J.B. Priestley.

8) In what way does the Inspector behave like a playwright within the play?

9) When and where was the play first performed?

In-depth Questions

1) How could a naturalistic set design be used to establish the setting of *An Inspector Calls*? Explain your answer.

2) Explain how the Birlings' social status might influence your costume design for Sybil Birling.

3) How could a director use staging to reflect how gender stereotypes are challenged during the play?

4) How might the actor playing Mrs Birling emphasise the way her age affects her views and willingness to change? Explain your answer.

5) How might a director emphasise the connection between the Inspector and J.B. Priestley?

6) As a director, what themes would you try to emphasise to make a production of the play relevant to a modern audience? Explain your answer.

Practice Questions

Now you should know the context and themes of 'An Inspector Calls' inside-out and upside-down, so it's time to have a go at some longer questions. This type of question will be worth more marks in the exam, so make sure you answer them properly.

Exam-style Questions

> Find the part of Act One where Mr Birling, Gerald and Eric are talking in the dining room. Read from where Eric says **"What's the joke? Started telling stories?"** to where the Inspector says **"Quite so"**, then answer Question 1 below.

1) Imagine you're directing a production of *An Inspector Calls*. Explain how you would use costume to portray this extract effectively on stage to the audience. You should refer to the play's context in your answer.

> Find the part of Act Three where Mr and Mrs Birling and Gerald decide to phone the infirmary. Read from where Gerald says **"I don't mind doing it"** to the end of the play, then answer Question 2 below.

2) Imagine you're directing a production of *An Inspector Calls*. Explain how you would use props and stage furniture to portray this extract effectively on stage to the audience. You should refer to the play's context in your answer.

> Find the part of Act Three where the Inspector is about to make his final exit. Read from where the Inspector says **"You're offering the money at the wrong time"** to where Mr Birling says **"Any more of that and you leave this room"**, then answer Questions 3 and 4 below.

3) Imagine you're directing a production of *An Inspector Calls*. Explain how you would use staging to portray this extract effectively to the audience. You should refer to the play's context in your answer.

4) Imagine you're directing a production of *An Inspector Calls*. Explain how you would use props and stage furniture to portray this extract effectively to the audience. You should refer to the play's context in your answer.

Genre and Structure

An Inspector Calls borrows features from several theatrical genres — read on to learn more.

'An Inspector Calls' has elements of different genres

1) A play's genre refers to the type of story it tells. *An Inspector Calls* combines elements of different genres, notably well-made plays, morality plays and crime thrillers.

2) A director might choose to emphasise one particular genre over another using performance and design choices. The genre the director focuses on could affect how the audience interprets the play.

3) For example, emphasising aspects of the crime thriller genre may make the play feel more tense, whereas focusing on elements of the morality play genre may make the audience think about their own flaws.

It could be considered a well-made play

1) When people describe *An Inspector Calls* as a well-made play, they're not just giving Priestley a compliment — they're referring to a genre of play that developed in the nineteenth century.

2) *An Inspector Calls* contains elements of a well-made play, but it doesn't fit the genre exactly.

In a typical well-made play, some of the 'action' has taken place before the play begins, and the first part of the play sets up the situation the characters will face.	At the start of the play, Eva/Daisy has already died. The Inspector arriving to question the characters establishes the situation the play will explore.

Like a typical well-made play, An Inspector Calls has a deliberate structure — each scene gradually reveals more information and builds tension.

Well-made plays build suspense, often because of misunderstandings or hidden information, which the audience may know even if the characters don't.	The hidden information is that all the characters are connected to Eva/Daisy, and they all contributed to her death. However, only the Inspector knows this — the audience find out at the same time as the characters.
Letters or diaries might be used in a well-made play to reveal the truth.	The Inspector refers to Eva/Daisy's diary, which gives him information about the Birlings' past behaviour. The Inspector's photo of Eva/Daisy also helps reveal each character's connection to her.
A well-made play uses a series of revelations to move the plot forwards. The ending then explains the situation established at the start and resolves all the problems that have occurred.	Each character's involvement in Eva/Daisy's death becomes clear through a series of revelations. In the last act, the family's problems seem resolved when Gerald discovers that Inspector Goole isn't a real police inspector. However, the phone call at the end suggests that their problems aren't over — this final twist isn't typical of well-made plays.

It shares features with morality plays

1) Morality plays are religious dramas that were popular in the sixteenth century. The main characters were often guilty of one of the seven deadly sins. The plays were performed to warn people about the dangers of these sins and encourage them to change their ways.

2) *An Inspector Calls* contains some elements of a morality play. The characters are each guilty of one or more of the seven deadly sins (e.g. Mr Birling is guilty of greed, Mrs Birling is guilty of pride) and the Inspector tries to get them to confess and repent.

'repenting' is the act of feeling sorry for committing a sin.

3) However, unlike traditional morality plays, there's no religion involved. The moral judge isn't God, but a police inspector.

4) Highlighting the play's morality play aspects would make the Inspector's message seem more important, as it would encourage the audience to think about how their own 'sinful' behaviour can affect others.

Genre and Structure

It's similar to a crime thriller

1) <u>Crime thrillers</u> revolve around a <u>crime</u> — often a <u>mysterious murder</u> — and the process of <u>solving</u> it.

2) In crime thrillers, the crime itself isn't the <u>climax</u> of the story — instead it <u>drives</u> the <u>rest of the action</u>. The story gradually reveals <u>how</u> the crime occurred and '<u>whodunnit</u>'.

3) In *An Inspector Calls*, Eva/Daisy's death is a <u>suicide</u>, but Priestley suggests she was <u>driven</u> to killing herself because of the way people treated her — the Birling family and Gerald are all <u>suspects</u>.

4) Unlike in traditional crime thrillers, <u>no one</u> is ultimately held <u>accountable</u> for Eva/Daisy's death.

5) Instead, Priestley takes the revelations of the play <u>one step further</u> by suggesting that <u>everyone in society</u> is to <u>blame</u> for the suffering of people like Eva/Daisy.

© Donald Cooper/REX/Shutterstock

The play's structure creates tension

1) Elements of *An Inspector Calls'* <u>structure</u> help to build <u>tension</u> for the audience.

2) For example, *An Inspector Calls* is made up of <u>three acts</u>. Three-act plays <u>usually</u> follow this format:

| Act One <u>introduces the characters</u>. | → | Act Two <u>develops these characters</u> and builds up to a <u>climax</u>. | → | Act Three <u>relieves the tension</u> and brings the action to a <u>close</u>. |

3) *An Inspector Calls* shares <u>some</u> of the features of a traditional three-act structure. Act One <u>introduces the characters</u>, while Act Two <u>develops the characters</u> and ends with a <u>climax</u> — the revelation that Eva/Daisy was <u>pregnant</u> with Eric's baby.

There's more about structure and tension on p. 23.

4) Act Three seems to <u>relieve the tension</u> when the characters realise that Inspector Goole <u>wasn't a real police Inspector</u>, and that there's <u>no report</u> of a suicide.

5) However, the phone call at the end of the play <u>increases the tension</u>, and ends the play with a <u>cliffhanger</u>. Unlike a typical three-act play, *An Inspector Calls* <u>doesn't</u> end with a neat resolution.

6) Priestley also creates tension by having the <u>amount of time</u> that passes for the characters be the <u>same</u> as the time it takes to <u>perform</u> the play — the action flows <u>continuously</u> between acts. This makes the events feel <u>real</u> for the audience and maintains the feeling of <u>suspense</u> — the whole of the play focuses on one <u>intense</u> situation.

7) There are no moments of <u>comic relief</u> to <u>distract</u> the audience from the Inspector's <u>interrogation</u> of the characters either — the tension is almost <u>relentless</u>.

The structure suggests that events might repeat themselves

1) The <u>phone call</u> at the end of the play announcing the imminent arrival of a police inspector makes it seems like the events in the play might <u>happen again</u>. This suggests that the characters won't be free from <u>accusations</u> until they <u>change their ways</u> and <u>accept responsibility</u> for their actions.

2) The play's <u>ending</u> encourages the audience to <u>consider</u> how the Birlings will react the <u>second time</u> they are questioned and whether they will <u>learn from the past</u>.

An Inspector Calls is like camping — it's intense...

If you're asked to write about how you would direct an extract of *An Inspector Calls* in the exam, think about how the play's genre and structure might influence decisions about performance and design.

Style

A play's style is usually decided by the director (the power, mwahaha...).

'An Inspector Calls' could be staged in a naturalistic style...

1) Naturalism is a style of theatre that aims to recreate real life on stage. The play should seem real to the audience and they should be able to forget that they're in a theatre. This means every aspect of the performance has to be believable, including the scenery, lighting and sound.

2) In the stage directions, Priestley suggests that the play should be staged naturalistically, noting that it takes place in 1912 and in "*The dining-room of a fairly large suburban house*". Using authentic furniture and clothing would help convey this setting and time period accurately to the audience.

This production used a naturalistic style.

3) The language used in the play also echoes real dialogue from 1912, e.g. the characters use words like "squiffy" and "By Jingo!". This helps to give the audience a stronger sense of the time period of the play.

4) Priestley doesn't specify any special effects in his stage directions. This makes it easier to achieve a naturalistic style. A director could consider how to make the lighting seem natural within the play — they could choose to use lamps within the set rather than large overhead lights to realistically create the "*pink and intimate*" lighting described by Priestley in his opening stage directions.

... or a director could choose a non-naturalistic style

1) Non-naturalistic productions include features that make the audience more aware that what they're watching isn't real.

> The 'fourth wall' is the imagined barrier between the actors on stage and the audience.

2) A non-naturalistic production might break the fourth wall by including elements that remind the audience that they're watching a play, for example by having characters enter the stage through the aisles of the theatre.

3) In the instructions for the set design, Priestley suggests that a director could "*dispense with an ordinary realistic set*" — he realised *An Inspector Calls* could also lend itself to a non-naturalistic style.

- A 1992 production of *An Inspector Calls*, directed by Stephen Daldry, used a false proscenium arch (see p. 50). The curtain of this arch would fall down at specific moments, and then be put back in place by the characters on stage. This deliberately broke the fourth wall, drawing the audience's attention to the fact that they were watching a play.

- Daldry also altered the time the play was set in to emphasise key ideas, setting it partly in 1912 and partly in wartime 1945. A massive 'dolls' house' in the centre of the stage represented 1912, with the walls opening up to reveal an early 20th-century dining room. Wartime 1945 was represented by street lamps, a telephone box, and a crowd of people dressed in 1940s clothes. These images of Britain after a long war emphasised the opportunity Priestley might have seen to rebuild society in a more fair and equal way.

EXAM TIP

Knots, split ends — my hairstyle is pretty naturalistic...

A combination of a naturalistic and non-naturalistic style could be used. The key thing is to consider how the different aspects of the production, e.g. the stage design or lighting, might all add to the play's style.

Mood and Atmosphere

Mood and atmosphere can have a big impact on the audience, so they should be considered carefully.

The setting helps create a claustrophobic atmosphere

1) All the action takes place in <u>one location</u> — the Birlings' dining room. This creates a feeling of <u>claustrophobia</u> and makes the audience feel <u>on edge</u> — there's no <u>relief</u> from the tension in the room.

2) The one-room setting also suggests that the Birlings have been living in their own <u>protected bubble</u>, <u>unaware</u> of the problems faced by other members of society. The Inspector <u>bursts</u> this bubble and makes it <u>impossible</u> for the characters to hide from the <u>consequences</u> of their actions.

The mood on stage changes

1) The <u>mood</u> at the start of the play is <u>relaxed</u>, but it becomes more <u>tense</u> when the Inspector arrives.

2) This tension <u>continues</u> until after the Inspector's departure in Act Three. When the characters discover that Goole wasn't a <u>real police inspector</u> and that <u>no one</u> has died, Mr and Mrs Birling <u>relax</u> — they are described as "*smiling*" and speaking "*jovially*".

3) The <u>pause</u> in tension towards the end of Act Three helps to make the phone call at the end of the play even more <u>shocking</u>.

© Marilyn Kingwill / ArenaPAL

Structure is used to build tension

1) Priestley <u>increases tension</u> in the play by having the Inspector <u>release information bit-by-bit</u>. He shows the photo to <u>one person</u> at a time and positions himself so the others <u>can't see</u> — the characters, like the audience, are kept <u>on their toes</u>.

2) Priestley also uses the <u>beginnings and ends of acts</u> to maintain the tense atmosphere:

- Act One ends with the Inspector asking "<u>Well?</u>". Act Two opens with the <u>same moment</u>. <u>Freezing</u> the action in this way makes the audience <u>wonder</u> about his question <u>during the pause</u>, creating <u>suspense</u>.

- At the beginning of Act Two, the audience <u>expects</u> the story to move on to <u>Gerald's confession</u>. But instead, Priestley <u>delays</u> the action by <u>shifting</u> the audience's attention to <u>Sybil and Sheila</u>. This <u>builds suspense</u> and increases the audience's <u>curiosity</u>.

- At the very end of Act Two, Eric <u>returns</u>. A director could increase tension here by including an <u>interval</u> between acts. This would create a <u>cliffhanger</u> by making the audience <u>wait</u> to hear <u>Eric's confession</u>.

- Even at the end of the play the tension <u>isn't relieved</u> — Act Three ends with a <u>shocking twist</u> which leaves the audience in <u>suspense</u>.

REVISION TASK

As if this exam didn't cause enough tension...

Write a paragraph about a key moment in 'An Inspector Calls' to explain how you might emphasise its mood or atmosphere if you were staging it. You should mention:

1) The things about that part of the play that suggest this mood or atmosphere.

2) How you would emphasise this particular mood or atmosphere.

3) The effect of your ideas on the audience.

Tick list:
✓ interpreting the play
✓ specific examples of how a mood is created
✓ effect on audience

Speech and Language

A play is nothing without words (literally...), but how the characters speak and the language they use also matters. It says a lot about who they are, their relationships and how (or if) they change during the play.

The way the characters speak reveals a lot about them

Speech can be used to give details about the characters, including their class, age and personality.

Class

- The Birlings and Gerald frequently use words that were common among the middle and upper classes in 1912, for example "chap" and "crank". This makes their speech seem more realistic to the audience.

- Mrs Birling and Gerald could speak using Received Pronunciation. This high-status accent would suggest that they're members of the upper classes. Mr Birling, on the other hand, might have a slight regional accent — this would hint that he is from a lower social class. This would highlight his hypocrisy — he is trying to improve his own social status, but he doesn't care about improving the lives of his factory staff by paying them more.

- Edna has a lower social status, and she has very few lines in the play. The language she uses is related to her position as a servant, e.g. "Yes, ma'am", "Please, sir". This highlights how working-class people didn't have a voice in society at this time.

Age

- The younger characters' use of slang from 1912 shows an age gap — Mrs Birling is shocked by Sheila's use of the word "squiffy".

- Gerald is from a higher social class than Mr Birling, but because he is younger, he speaks to Birling respectfully, frequently calling him "sir".

Personality

- Mr Birling uses language related to business, for example he calls the "hoax" an "elaborate sell". This suggests he lacks compassion — he sees things from a business perspective, rather than a human perspective.

- The Birlings and Gerald use euphemisms — vague words used to avoid saying something more unpleasant. E.g. Gerald says "women of the town" rather than 'prostitutes'. Using euphemisms shows they want to appear respectable and not admit that they know about things like prostitution.

The Inspector's speech is different

1) The Inspector's speech sets him apart from the other characters. He uses language to force confessions from the Birlings, as well as using language to try to change the way they think and behave towards others.

2) Using emotive language allows him to attempt to create an emotional response from the characters and the audience. Describing Eva as a "pretty" and "lively" girl helps to create sympathy for her.

3) He uses blunt, graphic language, e.g. describing how the bleach killed Eva/Daisy — "Burnt her inside out". This is shocking, and contrasts with the Birlings' use of euphemisms to avoid reality.

4) He refuses to follow social rules in his speech. Rather than speaking to the Birlings respectfully, he interrogates them aggressively until they confess. This shows how someone's class isn't important to him.

5) Often, he answers his own questions — e.g. when Sybil refuses to admit there was a committee meeting, he says, "You know very well there was". This reinforces his omniscience — he already knows everything the characters will tell him.

6) His use of silence is unusual — he has a "disconcerting habit" of staring at someone before speaking to them. This makes them feel uneasy, giving him power over them.

Effect on the Audience

An actor playing the Inspector could speak quietly at reflective moments, e.g. when he describes Eva/Daisy's "fresh start" when she gets the job at Milwards. This might make him seem more compassionate to the audience.

Speech and Language

Speech can reveal more about a character's personality

1) Priestley uses <u>different kinds</u> of speech to show <u>relationships</u> between characters.

> • **Dialogue** is the general term for <u>speech</u> between the characters <u>on stage</u>.
> • A **duologue** is when <u>two characters</u> have a conversation together.
> • A **monologue** is when a character makes a <u>speech</u> to the audience or another character.

2) Mr Birling gives a number of <u>monologues</u> in Act One. They establish him as a <u>self-important</u> character, and suggest that he tends to <u>talk</u> rather than <u>listen</u>.

3) When the Inspector arrives, he <u>questions</u> the characters in a series of <u>duologues</u>. Focussing his questions on <u>one character</u> at a time makes them feel <u>vulnerable</u> and <u>isolated</u>, which gives the Inspector more <u>power</u>. He <u>intimidates</u> each character and forces them to <u>confess</u> in front of other family members.

4) Sheila and Gerald share a <u>duologue</u> at the end of Act One and Gerald reveals he <u>knew Daisy</u>. The conversation shows a <u>shift</u> in their relationship — Sheila is now <u>in control</u> as she <u>interrogates</u> Gerald.

5) The <u>warning</u> that the Inspector gives before his final exit in Act Three is a <u>monologue</u>. It might be directed either at the other <u>characters</u> on stage or at the <u>audience</u> — directing it at the audience would encourage them to think about how the Inspector's message <u>relates to their own lives</u>.

6) After the revelation that Goole <u>isn't a real inspector</u> in Act Three, the family start to <u>argue</u> — they <u>interrupt</u> each other and talk "*angrily*" and "*scornfully*". This <u>chaotic</u> dialogue <u>contrasts</u> with the amicable dialogue at the start of Act One and shows how the Inspector's visit has <u>fractured</u> the family's relationships.

> **Physical skills**
>
> The performers could reinforce the <u>chaotic dialogue</u> in Act Three by using their <u>physical skills</u>. Moving <u>quickly</u> or going <u>closer</u> to one another could highlight the <u>conflict</u> in the family.

Language can show a change in a character

1) In Act One, Sheila's language is <u>childish and submissive</u>, e.g. "I'm sorry, Daddy." Later, she is more <u>confident</u> and <u>assertive</u>, and this is reinforced by her <u>blunt</u> language, e.g. "we drove that girl to commit suicide." This shows how she <u>matures</u> throughout the play.

2) At the start of the play, Eric speaks in an <u>uncontrolled</u>, sometimes <u>rude</u>, manner, e.g. <u>suddenly exclaiming</u> "Steady the Buffs!". At the end of the play, he is more <u>assertive</u>, challenging his parents about the family's <u>responsibility</u> for Eva/Daisy's death, e.g. stating "We did her in all right."

3) Mr Birling's language <u>doesn't really change</u>. He reverts back to giving <u>monologues</u> in Act Three, which suggests that he <u>hasn't learnt</u> from the Inspector's visit.

© Vishal Sharma/Altrincham Garrick Playhouse

REVISION TASK

Duologue — a conversation between two logs...

Choose a key moment from the play for one of the characters. Write a paragraph about how you would deliver their speech to show key ideas about the character. Remember to include:

1) The ideas you would convey about the character.
2) How you would use your vocal skills to do this.
3) The effect of these skills on the audience.

> Tick list:
> ✓ dramatic intentions
> ✓ vocal skills
> ✓ effect on audience

Stage Directions

Priestley puts a lot of information into the stage directions. They don't just tell the actors what to do and when — they also give information about lighting, scenery, props and the set.

Stage directions give useful information

A director could choose to ignore some or all of the stage directions to suit their production.

1) Priestley includes stage directions to guide performers and designers. These include instructions on speech, movement and gestures, as well as design elements like costume, lighting, scenery and props.

2) They're also used to specify the positioning of actors on stage.

3) Some stage directions give a straightforward instruction, e.g. "Birling *stops to listen.*" Others are more descriptive and open to the actor's interpretation, e.g. "*she stares at him wonderingly and dubiously.*"

They can control the pace of the action

1) Priestley carefully times characters' entrances and exits — e.g. Mrs Birling enters in Act Two just as the Inspector and Sheila are having an intense conversation. This suddenly slows the pace, but also creates tension, as the audience realises Mrs Birling doesn't know what the other characters were discussing.

2) Act Two ends suddenly — the "*Curtain falls quickly*". The suddenness interrupts the emotional intensity at this point, and creates tension by not letting the story continue until the next act.

3) The stage directions also indicate the speed at which lines should be delivered. When the Inspector explains "*rather slowly*" that Eva/Daisy "didn't exactly" go onto the streets in Act One, he controls the pace of the action and hints that he knows more about what happened than he's letting on.

They reveal characters' emotions and motivations

1) The stage directions sometimes tell a performer which emotion to express when saying a line. The Inspector often speaks "*sternly*" to the characters. This shows that he wants the characters to listen to him and that he is trying to teach them to behave in a better way.

2) When Mr Birling speaks "*triumphantly*" after Gerald calls the hospital in Act Three, the actor should speak loudly and happily — this suggests that Mr Birling is glad that all his problems are all over.

Stage directions add to the play's subtext

1) Stage directions can hint at hidden motivations and information — they reveal things that aren't spoken in the dialogue.

2) For example, when Sheila teases Gerald about his absence last summer, the actor should be "*half serious, half playful*". This suggests that Sheila is suspicious of Gerald's behaviour.

3) The stage directions also provide insights into the characters' behaviour. Eric is "*uneasy*" in Act One — this hints that he could be hiding something from the other characters.

© Vishal Sharma/Altrincham Garrick Playhouse

Student exits exam hall, smiling smugly to themselves...

The stage directions suggest how Priestley imagined the characters feeling at particular points. Think about how an actor could use their physical and vocal skills to communicate this to the audience.

Practice Questions

Finally, it's your time to shine. Put pen to paper and have a go at this page of practice questions to check how much you've learnt about Priestley's techniques in the play.

Quick Questions

1) *An Inspector Calls* has features of a crime thriller and a morality play.
   For each of these genres, give one example of a similarity from the play.

2) How does Priestley use structure to suggest that the events of the play might repeat themselves?

3) Is breaking the fourth wall a naturalistic or non-naturalistic feature of theatre?

4) What is the effect of setting the play in one room?

5) Give an example of how tension is built up during the play.

6) How is Edna's working-class status shown through her language?

7) Give two aspects of the Inspector's style of speech that set him apart from the other characters.

8) What is the difference between a monologue and a duologue?

9) Give an example from Act One of Sheila using childish language.

10) Give an example of a stage direction which helps control the pace of the action.

In-depth Questions

1) Describe how the atmosphere of Act One changes after the Inspector arrives.

2) If you were directing a production of *An Inspector Calls*, would you use a naturalistic or non-naturalistic style? Explain your answer.

3) Write a paragraph explaining how Mr Birling's use of language in Act One establishes his character to the audience.

4) Imagine that you are performing the role of Eric. Explain how you would use vocal and physical skills in your performance to create an uneasy atmosphere in Act One.

5) The character notes about Gerald Croft say that he is *"very much the easy well-bred young man-about-town."* How might this information help an actor to portray the character?

Practice Questions

Still hungry for more practice? Well, it's time to tuck into some meaty exam-style questions. You'll need a copy of the play and some blank paper before you get started.

Exam-style Questions

> Read Act One from where Mr Birling says **"Cigar?"** to where Mr Birling says **"I wanted you to have the benefit of my experience"**, then answer Questions 1 and 2.

1) Imagine you're a director staging a production of *An Inspector Calls*. Discuss how you would use staging to bring this extract to life for your audience. You should refer to the context in which the text was written and performed.

2) Imagine you're a director staging a production of *An Inspector Calls*. Explain how a performer playing the character of Gerald might demonstrate his high status to the audience in this extract and elsewhere in the play. You should talk about performance skills, stage directions and use of stage space in your answer.

> Find the part of Act One just before the Inspector shows Sheila the photograph. Read from where the Inspector says **"There are a lot of young women living that sort of existence"** to where he says **"All in good time."**, then answer Question 3 below.

3) Imagine you're directing a production of *An Inspector Calls*. Explain how you would use props and stage furniture to make the revelation of new information effective for the audience. In your answer, you should refer to the play's context.

> Find the part of Act Three where the Inspector is questioning Eric. Read from where Sheila and Mrs Birling re-enter the scene to where the Inspector says **"Good night."** and leaves the stage, then answer Questions 4 and 5 below.

4) Imagine you're playing the role of Eric. Describe how you would use your vocal performance to show how Eric feels throughout this extract.

5) Imagine you're a sound designer for a production of *An Inspector Calls*. Explain how you would use sound to enhance the tense atmosphere in this extract.

Character Performance — The Inspector

There aren't loads of characters in *An Inspector Calls*, which means that they're all pretty important. So let's dive in with the character who gives his name to the title — good ol' Inspector Goole...

The Inspector is a mysterious character

1) Inspector Goole is introduced as a police <u>detective</u>, but the other characters and the audience don't learn much about who he <u>actually</u> is.

2) His <u>identity</u> is called into question at the <u>end</u> of the play when the Birlings <u>discover</u> that there's no-one called <u>Goole</u> working for the <u>Brumley</u> police force.

3) The Inspector is an <u>outsider</u>. He doesn't share the Birlings' <u>values</u> or belong to the <u>class system</u> that they live in. His costume of a "*plain darkish suit*" also doesn't give many clues about who he is.

4) As his <u>true identity</u> is never made clear, it's been suggested he could represent many <u>different</u> things. For instance, his <u>mysterious nature</u> and his almost <u>supernatural</u> knowledge of the Birlings' lives makes him seem like a sort of <u>ghost</u>. The name Inspector Goole also plays on the words '<u>spectre</u>' and '<u>ghoul</u>'.

5) The Inspector could also <u>represent</u> the Birlings' <u>consciences</u>, telling them what they've done wrong, or he could be interpreted as a <u>mouthpiece</u> for <u>J.B. Priestley</u> (see p. 15).

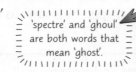
'spectre' and 'ghoul' are both words that mean 'ghost'.

© Mark Douet / ArenaPAL

> **The Inspector is...**
>
> **moral:** "We are responsible for each other."
> **purposeful:** "It's my duty to ask questions"
> **authoritative:** "Come along, Mr Croft. What happened?"

He's an authoritative figure

1) The Inspector <u>drives</u> most of the <u>action</u> on stage through his <u>questioning</u> of the other characters.

2) He is very <u>purposeful</u> — he <u>doesn't stop</u> questioning the Birlings until the <u>truth</u> has been revealed.

3) The Inspector speaks "*sternly*" and "*sharply*" to the Birlings, but doesn't <u>lose control</u> of himself like they do.

4) He <u>isn't afraid</u> of <u>upsetting</u> or <u>offending</u> the other characters. Unlike the Birlings, he doesn't care about <u>social conventions</u>.

5) The Inspector's <u>not influenced</u> or <u>intimidated</u> by Mr Birling, despite Mr Birling's attempts to <u>flatter</u> and <u>threaten</u> him — instead he <u>interrupts</u> Mr Birling and makes <u>sarcastic remarks</u>.

> **Effect on the Audience**
>
> It's up to the <u>performer</u> to use the <u>stage directions</u> and their <u>own skills</u> effectively to make the Inspector seem <u>powerful</u> to the audience from the start.

6) An actor playing the Inspector could <u>raise</u> the <u>volume</u> of their <u>voice</u> and <u>speak slowly</u> and <u>deliberately</u> to show the Inspector's <u>authority</u> over the other characters.

He's concerned with morals and caring for others

1) The Inspector asks the Birlings and Gerald about how they <u>each contributed</u> to Eva/Daisy's death, but he's <u>most interested</u> in making them see the <u>error</u> of their ways — he seems to know the facts <u>already</u>.

2) Before his <u>final exit</u>, he gives a <u>speech</u> about how everyone in society has to <u>look after each other</u> — it's the <u>opposite</u> of <u>Mr Birling's speech</u> in Act One about how a man has to "<u>look after himself and his own</u>".

3) He's <u>on Eva/Daisy's side</u> throughout the play and sees his role as being to <u>argue</u> on behalf of the <u>poor</u> and <u>powerless</u> in the face of abuse and neglect from the <u>wealthy and powerful</u>. For example, he speaks passionately about mistreatment of the "<u>millions of Eva Smiths and John Smiths</u>" in society.

Character Performance — The Inspector

He's physically imposing

1) The stage directions describe the Inspector as giving off a sense of "*massiveness, solidity and purposefulness*", though Priestley says that he "*need not be a big man*". This suggests that it is the way the Inspector moves and holds himself that gives this sense, rather than his physical size.

2) An actor playing the Inspector could use stillness to create a sense of "*solidity*", e.g. when he's listening to someone answering his questions, he could remain very still to suggest that he is determined to hear their confession.

3) To create a sense of "*purposefulness*", an actor could make slow and deliberate movements, e.g. when looking at different characters or flipping through his notebook. This would suggest that he is very focused on his task.

4) In Act One, the Inspector obstructs Eric and Gerald when they try to see the photograph he's showing to Mr Birling. An actor playing the Inspector could do this by stepping in front of them without looking at them. This use of his physicality would show how the Inspector is able to control others effortlessly.

A square stance and stern expression help to make this Inspector seem imposing.

Effect on the Audience

Even though the play's title suggests an inspector will arrive, the audience are likely to be unsettled by his entrance because it is so unexpected. An actor could reinforce this by using physical and vocal skills to seem more intimidating.

The Inspector takes charge in Act One

1) When the Inspector enters the Birlings' home in Act One, he becomes the most powerful and authoritative figure on stage.

2) He asserts his dominance over Mr Birling and then questions him and Sheila about their parts in Eva/Daisy's fate. The Inspector seems very calm and collected during Act One.

Act One — Physical Skills

- The Inspector has the habit of "*looking hard*" at people before speaking to them. Prolonged eye contact could suggest that he is scrutinising the characters and isn't afraid to be impolite.

- The Inspector could sit opposite Mr Birling, so that when he questions him, the audience are reminded of a police interview, emphasising the Inspector's authority and Birling's guilt.

- When the Inspector shows Sheila the photograph of Eva/Daisy under a lamp, "*she crosses to him*". An actor playing the Inspector could walk purposefully over to the lamp without looking back to force Sheila to follow him. This would emphasise how much control the Inspector has.

Act One — Vocal Skills

- The Inspector gives several distressing lines about Eva/Daisy, e.g. saying that the disinfectant "Burnt her inside out". An actor could deliver these lines in an unemotional, matter-of-fact tone. This would show that the Inspector isn't afraid of facing the truth, unlike the Birlings, and that he wants to shock them into understanding how serious the situation is.

- Unlike her father, Sheila does show remorse, and so the Inspector isn't as harsh towards her. He doesn't lose his temper, but isn't sympathetic to her either. An actor might use a calm, even tone when talking to Sheila to reflect this.

Character Performance — The Inspector

In Act Two, he continues his stern approach

1) The Inspector questions Gerald and Mrs Birling in Act Two — he's still <u>calm</u> and <u>collected</u>, but takes a <u>harsher approach</u> when Mrs Birling <u>won't cooperate</u>.

2) By the <u>end</u> of the act, the Inspector is still <u>in control</u> of the situation. This contrasts with Mr and Mrs Birling, who have become <u>distressed</u> and <u>frightened</u> by his questions.

Act Two — Physical Skills

- When the Inspector enters and <u>interrupts</u> Sheila and Gerald's conversation, an actor could <u>walk between</u> them, symbolising how his visit will drive them <u>apart</u>.
- When the Inspector "<i>holds up a hand</i>" to <u>silence</u> Sheila, he could do it <u>without looking</u> at her, to suggest that she is just a <u>distraction</u>.

Act Two — Vocal Skills

- An actor playing the Inspector could use a <u>sharp tone</u> when questioning Sybil to suggest that he is <u>irritated</u> by her <u>attitude</u>.
- At the <u>end</u> of the act, when the Inspector <u>repeats</u> the sorts of things Sybil has said ("<u>No hushing up, eh?</u>"), he could <u>mimic</u> her accent and intonation to show that he is <u>mocking</u> her.

The Inspector is at his most powerful in Act Three

1) The Inspector questions Eric with more <u>urgency</u> than the other characters, asking questions in quick succession. This intense interrogation makes the Inspector seem more <u>intimidating</u>.

2) When the Inspector makes his speech, the other characters have all been <u>quietened</u> by his revelations. This allows the Inspector to appear <u>more powerful</u> as he delivers his message about social responsibility.

Act Three — Vocal Skills

- When the Inspector <u>reminds</u> each of the Birlings that they are to <u>blame</u>, an actor could <u>place stress</u> on the word "<u>you</u>" so that he <u>sounds</u> more <u>accusatory</u>.
- An actor could <u>increase the volume</u> of his voice during the <u>speech</u> so that the <u>tension builds</u> to a <u>climax</u>, making his words more <u>frightening</u> and <u>dramatic</u>.
- During his <u>final speech</u>, an actor playing the Inspector could leave a <u>pause</u> after <u>each sentence</u> to give his words <u>weight</u>.

Act Three — Physical Skills

- An actor playing the Inspector could use an <u>upright posture</u> during his last speech to make himself appear more <u>imposing</u> and his message more <u>powerful</u>.
- He could also <u>furrow</u> his <u>brow</u> to make his message seem more <u>serious</u> and <u>important</u>.
- <u>Arm gestures</u> could be used to show whether he's addressing the <u>audience</u> or the other <u>actors</u>, e.g. he might hold his arms out <u>openly</u> toward the audience to show that he is <u>sincerely</u> urging them to <u>listen</u> to his lesson.

Effect on the Audience

<u>Addressing</u> the audience might cause them to <u>think</u> about their <u>own</u> actions in relation to the Inspector's <u>message</u>.

You can't fool the Goole, so don't even try...

Read Act Three from the Inspector's line "You're offering the money at the wrong time" until his exit. Write a few paragraphs about how you would perform this extract, making sure to cover:

1) How you would use your voice (e.g. pitch and tone).
2) How you would use body language, gestures and proxemics.
3) The effects of these choices on the audience.

Tick list:
- ✓ understanding of the play
- ✓ appropriate physical and vocal performance skills
- ✓ overall effect on audience

Character Performance — Arthur Birling

Arthur Birling is stubborn and self-centred — he doesn't think much of the Inspector and his principles. He's far more worried about public embarrassment or loss of wealth than he is about Eva/Daisy's death.

Arthur Birling is a prominent local businessman

1) Mr Birling is a <u>wealthy, successful businessman</u>. He <u>owns a factory</u> in Brumley.

2) He is Sheila and Eric's <u>father</u>, and is <u>married</u> to Sybil Birling — he's the <u>head of the family</u>.

3) He's <u>well-connected</u> in Brumley. He is friends with the <u>Chief Constable</u> and has served as the <u>Lord Mayor</u>. In Act One, he reveals that he is expecting to receive a <u>knighthood</u> soon.

©Vishal Sharma/Altrincham Garrick Playhouse

Arthur Birling is...

arrogant: "I was an alderman for years — and Lord Mayor two years ago"

uncompassionate: "if they didn't like those rates, they could go and work somewhere else."

foolish: "The Germans don't want war. Nobody wants war"

He only cares about himself

1) Mr Birling's <u>first concern</u> when the Inspector tells him about Eva/Daisy's death is whether it will cause him <u>public embarrassment</u> and cost him his <u>knighthood</u> — he's only worried about his <u>reputation</u>.

2) He doesn't show any <u>sympathy</u> for Eva/Daisy. When the Inspector describes how she died, he just says "Yes, yes. Horrible business." He <u>doesn't seem upset</u> about it.

- Mr Birling <u>doesn't believe</u> in the idea of <u>social responsibility</u> — that people in society have a <u>duty</u> to <u>look after</u> one another. In one of his early <u>speeches</u> he tells Eric and Gerald that a man has to "<u>look after himself and his own</u>".

- Mr Birling <u>admits</u> that he fired Eva/Daisy because she was asking for <u>higher wages</u>, but sees his actions as <u>justified</u> and <u>necessary</u> for the success of his business.

- Although he becomes <u>increasingly agitated</u> by the Inspector's <u>questions</u>, Mr Birling is <u>incapable of change</u> — he <u>refuses</u> to accept any <u>responsibility</u> for his behaviour.

He's secretly insecure about his social status

1) Mr Birling is from a <u>lower social class</u> than his wife (who's his "*social superior*") and Gerald. He tries to give the <u>impression</u> of being <u>well-bred</u>, but he's actually quite <u>insecure</u> about his <u>social position</u>.

2) The stage directions describe Birling as "*<u>somewhat provincial in his speech</u>*". An actor could speak with Received Pronunciation, but occasionally slip into a stronger <u>regional accent</u> (e.g. when he's <u>angry</u>) to imply that he's trying to seem of a <u>higher class</u> than he is.

3) Birling is keen to impress <u>Gerald</u>, who's upper class. An actor playing Mr Birling might <u>lean in</u> towards Gerald and use a <u>familiar tone of voice</u> to suggest he's trying to build a <u>closer relationship</u>. He might also mirror Gerald's <u>gestures</u> and <u>body language</u> to suggest that he wants to be more like him.

4) Even though Mr Birling enjoys a <u>comfortable lifestyle</u>, he still wants more <u>money</u> and <u>power</u>. He <u>hopes</u> to merge his business with Gerald's father's company — Mr Birling's <u>main competitor</u> — which would increase his <u>profits</u> as well as his <u>social standing</u>.

Effect on the Audience

Arthur <u>isn't</u> a <u>sympathetic</u> figure, but an actor could highlight his <u>insecurities</u>, which may make him more <u>relatable</u> to an audience.

Character Performance — Arthur Birling

He's middle-aged and has a large stature

1) Birling is described as being "*in his middle fifties*". An actor could reflect his <u>age</u> by moving around the stage a little <u>less</u> than the younger characters and by using slightly more <u>laboured gestures</u>. He could <u>sigh</u> when sitting down or standing up in order to suggest he is <u>less energetic</u> than the younger characters.

2) He is "*heavy-looking*", so a designer might add <u>padding</u> to his costume — an actor could draw the audience's attention to this by sitting with his hands <u>spread across his stomach</u>.

© Simon Gough Photography

3) An actor could reinforce Birling's <u>physicality</u> by <u>puffing out his chest</u> and walking with a <u>heavy stride</u>.

4) Mr Birling is also described as "*portentous*" ('pompous'), so an actor might <u>clear his throat</u> before <u>talking</u> to draw <u>everyone's attention</u> to what he has to say.

Mr Birling is in control at the start of Act One

1) <u>Before</u> the Inspector arrives, Mr Birling is <u>in control</u>. He gives <u>long speeches</u> about his own <u>opinions</u> and repeatedly offers <u>advice</u> to Gerald and Eric.

2) When the Inspector arrives, Mr Birling <u>loses</u> his position of <u>power</u>. He realises that the Inspector cannot be <u>flattered</u> or <u>intimidated</u> and he becomes increasingly <u>angry</u> and <u>defensive</u>.

Effect on the Audience

Birling could be performed in <u>different ways</u>. An actor may want to make his <u>arrogance</u> seem <u>pathetic or comical</u>, or they may want to perform him as a <u>cruel</u> and <u>ruthless</u> character.

Act One — Physical Skills

- An actor playing Birling could <u>stand</u> when he delivers his <u>monologues</u> to show how he's <u>comfortable</u> being the <u>centre of attention</u>. Using levels in this way also <u>forces</u> the other characters to <u>physically look up</u> at him, which would reinforce his position of <u>power</u> within the family.

- When Mr Birling talks <u>optimistically</u> about the future, an actor could <u>nudge</u> the character beside him to suggest that he expects the others to show signs of <u>agreement</u> with everything he's saying. This would highlight his <u>arrogant, pompous nature</u>.

- When the Inspector questions Mr Birling, an actor could use <u>closed body language</u> to show that he's <u>defensive</u>, e.g. <u>crossing his arms</u> or <u>turning away</u> from the Inspector.

- An actor could <u>shake his head</u> and <u>tut disapprovingly</u> when the Inspector says "There are a lot of young women living that sort of existence" to show his <u>lack of compassion</u> for Eva/Daisy.

Act One — Vocal Skills

- When Eric tries to speak during Mr Birling's <u>monologue</u>, Mr Birling <u>cuts him off</u> ("Just let me finish, Eric."). An actor playing Mr Birling could <u>raise the volume</u> of his voice and speak this line with a <u>faster pace</u> to show his <u>irritation</u> at being <u>interrupted</u>.

- An actor could use a <u>patronising tone</u> of voice when he speaks to Sybil or Sheila to highlight the way the <u>gender roles</u> work in the family (e.g. "Are you listening, Sheila? This concerns you too."). Mr Birling feels he's <u>better informed</u> and <u>more important</u> than the <u>women</u>.

- When he feels he's being <u>disrespected</u>, Mr Birling speaks "*angrily*" and "*abruptly*" to the Inspector. An actor could emphasise this when he delivers the line "<u>Look here, Inspector</u>" by <u>raising</u> the <u>volume</u> of his <u>voice</u> and <u>spitting out</u> the word "Inspector".

Character Performance — Arthur Birling

He becomes more anxious in Act Two

1) Mr Birling spends most of Act Two <u>worried</u> and <u>concerned</u>, and he makes a couple of <u>unsuccessful</u> attempts to <u>argue</u> with the Inspector.

2) By the end of the act, Mr Birling is "<u>*terrified*</u>" at the idea that Eric was also involved with Eva/Daisy, and that Eric was the father of her unborn child.

Act Two — Vocal Skills

- Mr Birling <u>tries</u> and <u>fails</u> to reassert his <u>authority</u> with the Inspector ("You'll apologise at once."). An actor could deliver his lines at a <u>higher pitch</u> to show that Mr Birling is <u>less sure</u> of himself.
- The Inspector tells Mr Birling not to "stammer and yammer", suggesting that Birling's <u>speech</u> has become <u>less confident</u>. An actor could <u>stutter</u> or <u>falter</u> over lines to reflect this.

Act Two — Physical Skills

- When Birling "<u>angrily</u>" tells the Inspector "Look here, I'm not going to have this", an actor could get quite <u>close</u> to the Inspector and <u>shake their finger</u> at him in an attempt to seem more <u>intimidating</u>.
- An actor could become <u>very still</u> at the end of the act when he's "<u>*thunderstruck*</u>" by what Eric has done. This would communicate his <u>shock</u> and <u>fear</u> to the audience.

Mr Birling returns to his old self by the end of Act Three

1) In the first part of Act Three, Mr Birling is still <u>worried</u> about the possibility of a <u>scandal</u>. He's also <u>very angry</u> with Eric for <u>stealing</u> from his company.

2) When Mr Birling begins to think the visit was a <u>trick</u>, he <u>returns</u> to how he was <u>before</u>. He's <u>triumphant</u> and <u>arrogant</u>, which shows he <u>hasn't learnt</u> his lesson.

Effect on the Audience

Birling's <u>unwillingness</u> to change may <u>frustrate</u> the audience. The fact that he has <u>power</u> in the local community doesn't give the audience much hope that the lives of the <u>less fortunate</u> will <u>improve</u>.

Act Three — Physical Skills

- When Mr Birling asks Eric why he didn't <u>ask for help</u>, Eric tells him he's "not the kind of father a chap could go to when he's in trouble". An actor playing Mr Birling might show this <u>emotional distance</u> by <u>standing apart</u> from Eric and using <u>closed body language</u> such as <u>crossing his arms</u>.
- Mr Birling is "<u>*the only active one*</u>" after the Inspector delivers his <u>final</u> speech. The actor playing Mr Birling could <u>wring his hands</u> or <u>fidget</u> with his <u>cuffs</u> as he goes to get a drink to show that he is <u>still unnerved</u> and <u>worried</u> about the <u>revelations</u>.

Act Three — Vocal Skills

- When the Inspector is questioning Eric, the stage directions describe Mr Birling speaking, "<u>*harshly*</u>" and "<u>*angrily*</u>" to the Inspector. An actor could speak in a <u>sharp tone</u> and place <u>greater emphasis</u> on words that show his <u>anger</u>.
- When Mr Birling <u>mimics</u> the Inspector with the line "<u>*You all helped to kill her*</u>", an actor could use an <u>exaggerated</u> version of the Inspector's <u>pitch</u>, <u>accent</u> and <u>inflection</u> to show that Mr Birling is now <u>relieved</u> and <u>confident</u> enough to <u>mock</u> the Inspector.

©Vishal Sharma/Altrincham Garrick Playhouse

©Vishal Sharma/Altrincham Garrick Playhouse

EXAM TIP

Head of the family? More like big-head of the family...

Birling may not seem complicated on the surface, but he's actually quite insecure — this makes him more interesting. Careful use of performance skills is key to reflect this so he doesn't seem one-dimensional.

Character Performance — Sybil Birling

Sybil Birling is a lot like her husband in many ways. She's self-important, unsympathetic to the less well-off and very concerned about maintaining her social standing. So much for opposites attracting...

Sybil is very traditional

1) Sybil Birling is the wife of Arthur, and mother to Sheila and Eric.

2) She's typical of middle-class women of the time. Because she's wealthy, she doesn't need to work and she has servants (Edna and "cook") to help her to run the household.

3) Mrs Birling has a lot of public influence. She runs a charitable organisation for women in Brumley. This organisation turned Eva/Daisy away when she came to them for help.

Sybil Birling is...

snobbish: "As if a girl of that sort would ever refuse money!"

stubborn: "you have no power to make me change my mind"

cowardly: "I don't think we need to discuss it"

She cares a lot about manners and social status

© Pete Jones / ArenaPAL

1) Mrs Birling is very concerned about people behaving in a socially acceptable way. Social conventions and class matter a lot to her — when Eva/Daisy comes to the charity and gives the name Mrs Birling, Sybil describes her behaviour as "gross impertinence".

2) She is offended by anyone who doesn't follow society's rules. She criticises her family for behaving inappropriately — "What an expression, Sheila".

3) As a member of a higher class, she expects to be treated with respect — she is outraged at the Inspector speaking bluntly to her.

4) She is very conscious of her reputation. She lies to the Inspector at first about not having known Eva/Daisy in order to protect herself from scandal.

5) She's also prejudiced towards people of a lower class than herself, e.g. she assumes that Eva/Daisy wouldn't refuse stolen money.

Sybil is dignified and unemotional

1) Mrs Birling is "*about fifty*" and is her "*husband's social superior*". An actor playing Mrs Birling could remain seated or move about the stage less than the younger characters to reflect her age. An actor could use Received Pronunciation to emphasise Mrs Birling's social status.

2) Middle-class women of the period were expected to be dignified and composed. An actor playing Mrs Birling could emphasise this by using an upright posture and keeping her hands folded in her lap — this might also show her pride.

3) Mrs Birling is confident and assertive — an actor playing her could demonstrate this by maintaining eye contact with other characters.

4) Sybil is described as "*a rather cold woman*". An actor could emphasise this lack of emotion by being distant towards her family, e.g. she could speak to Sheila and Eric haughtily, rather than warmly, or press her lips together tightly when one of her family members speaks out of turn.

Effect on the Audience

The more restrained and well-mannered Sybil is presented as being at the start of the play, the more surprised and shocked the audience are likely to be by her distress and loss of control later on.

Character Performance — Sybil Birling

In Act One she's formal and composed

1) Sybil Birling begins <u>confidently</u> in Act One, and <u>criticises</u> her family for their <u>poor manners</u>.

2) She <u>exits before</u> the Inspector <u>enters</u>, so she doesn't meet him in Act One.

Act One — Physical Skills

- Mrs Birling scolds Mr Birling when he <u>breaks social conventions</u>. An actor playing her could <u>widen their eyes</u> and clasp their <u>hand to their chest</u> when she says "Arthur, you're not supposed to say such things —" to show her <u>shock</u> and <u>disapproval</u>.

- Sybil is <u>warmer</u> with Gerald than any of the other characters, perhaps because he is <u>upper class</u>. When speaking to him, an actor could <u>smile</u> and pat his arm <u>affectionately</u>.

Act One — Vocal Skills

- Mrs Birling tries to sound <u>wise</u> when she <u>explains</u> to Sheila that she should <u>accept</u> that Gerald may often be too busy with work to see her. She could use a <u>matter-of-fact</u> or <u>patronising tone</u> to suggest that she thinks she <u>knows better</u> than Sheila.

- When she <u>interrupts</u> her husband's <u>long speech</u>, an actor could deliver the line "<u>Arthur!</u>" at a <u>louder volume</u> than her <u>usual</u> speech to show her <u>annoyance</u>.

Effect on the Audience

Mrs Birling <u>doesn't return</u> until partway through Act Two. An actor needs to give the audience a <u>strong sense</u> of her character in Act One so that her actions later <u>make sense</u>.

The Inspector's questions begin to distress her in Act Two

1) When Sybil enters in Act Two, she appears <u>confident</u>, but the Inspector's questions make her "<u>agitated</u>".

2) By the end of the act, Mrs Birling is <u>distraught</u> and <u>frightened</u> — she has <u>revealed</u> her part in Eva/Daisy's death and has <u>accidentally</u> incriminated Eric.

Effect on the Audience

Until this point, Sybil is <u>not</u> a <u>sympathetic</u> character. Showing her <u>vulnerability</u> would make her more <u>interesting</u> for the audience.

Act Two — Physical Skills

- When the Inspector agrees with Sheila and Mrs Birling exclaims "I beg your pardon!", an actor playing her could <u>look</u> the Inspector <u>up and down</u> in order to physically show her disapproval of his behaviour.

- When she is being <u>questioned</u>, an actor could react with <u>defensive body language</u>, e.g. <u>crossing her arms</u> or <u>leaning away</u> from the Inspector.

- When Mrs Birling realises she has <u>accidentally blamed Eric</u> for Eva/Daisy's death, her <u>distress</u> peaks. An actor could <u>shake</u> or try to <u>fight back tears</u> when delivering the line "But surely... I mean... it's ridiculous..." to show how she is so <u>frightened</u> that she has lost control.

© Simon Gough Photography

Act Two — Vocal Skills

- When she <u>introduces</u> herself to the Inspector with the line "I'm Mrs Birling, y'know", she could use <u>natural phrasing</u> and speak at a <u>slower pace</u> to show how <u>calm</u> and <u>confident</u> she feels.

- An actor playing Sybil could use a <u>sharp tone</u> to deliver the line "I don't know what you're talking about, Sheila" to show her <u>irritation</u> with her daughter for <u>siding</u> with the Inspector.

- Mrs Birling becomes <u>distressed</u> and "<u>cowed</u>" by the Inspector, an actor could <u>falter</u> over lines and use <u>longer pauses</u> to emphasise how <u>shocked</u> and <u>intimidated</u> she feels.

Character Performance — Sybil Birling

She doesn't really change during the play

1) Sybil begins Act Three in the same "_distressed_" manner as at the end of Act Two and continues to be <u>shocked</u> and <u>upset</u> during Eric's confessions to the Inspector.

2) Despite her <u>emotional reaction</u> to the Inspector's questioning, the change <u>isn't permanent</u>. When she <u>learns</u> that he wasn't a real police officer, she returns to her <u>old self</u>.

Act Three — Physical Skills

- An actor might use a <u>slack posture</u> and a <u>distraught facial expression</u> during the first part of Act Three to show that Mrs Birling feels <u>broken</u> by the Inspector's revelations.

- When she thinks that the Inspector might have been a hoax, an actor could <u>relax her posture</u>, <u>smile</u> and <u>move more freely</u> to suggest her <u>relief</u>. Sybil's <u>livelier behaviour</u> would <u>contrast</u> with her <u>restraint</u> earlier in the play, which would suggest that her emotions are <u>genuine</u>.

- Sybil's <u>animated</u> behaviour could <u>stop abruptly</u> when she <u>realises</u> an actual inspector is on the way. <u>Freezing still</u> in <u>shock</u> would emphasise the <u>change</u> in mood.

© Marilyn Kingwill / ArenaPAL

Sitting on the floor shows Mrs Birling's distress and loss of composure at the start of Act Three.

Act Three — Vocal Skills

- When Eric learns that Mrs Birling <u>turned Eva/Daisy away</u> from her charity, an actor playing her could deliver the line "No — Eric — please — I didn't know — I didn't understand —" at a <u>high pitch</u> and with a <u>strained tone</u> of voice to communicate her <u>distress</u> to the audience.

- Mrs Birling might be <u>frustrated</u> or <u>annoyed</u> that Eric and Sheila <u>aren't relieved</u> when it's revealed that the Inspector wasn't a real police officer. An actor could <u>sigh</u> in <u>exasperation</u> to reflect this.

- An actor playing Mrs Birling might <u>laugh unusually loudly</u> or for a little <u>too long</u> when Mr Birling does his <u>impression</u> of the Inspector, to suggest that her <u>relief</u> is causing her to find it <u>funnier</u> than she might do <u>ordinarily</u>.

Describe specific skills when writing about performance

When you write about <u>character performance</u>, think about the <u>overall effect</u> of <u>skills</u> on the audience:

> At the end of Act Two, when Mrs Birling realises that Eric is the father of Eva/Daisy's baby, I would show the character's shock by widening my eyes and dropping my jaw. Then, to show that she is struggling to make sense of what is happening, I would deliver the line "But surely... I mean... it's ridiculous..." in a shaky tone of voice, while physically trembling. This would make her shock and upset clear to the audience, and contrast with her previous, confident demeanour.

This describes the <u>effect</u> on the <u>audience</u> and shows awareness of Mrs Birling's <u>character arc</u>.

This makes a <u>clear point</u> and <u>describes</u> an appropriate <u>skill</u>.

This describes a <u>combination</u> of <u>physical</u> and <u>vocal</u> skills.

EXAM TIP

Sybil is stubborn, closed-minded, proud, self-serving...

... okay, I'm not being very charitable, but that makes two of us. Even though Mrs Birling isn't the nicest, it doesn't mean you have to play her as a wicked witch — consider how you could add depth to the role.

Character Performance — Sheila Birling

Unlike her parents, Sheila takes Inspector Goole's words to heart and changes a lot during the play. If the audience ends up liking any of the Birlings (and admittedly it's a stretch), it's probably going to be Sheila...

Sheila is a typical young middle-class woman

1) She is the daughter of Arthur and Sybil Birling, and the sister of Eric.
2) The stage directions describe her as "*a pretty girl in her early twenties*".
3) At the start of the play, the family are celebrating her engagement to Gerald Croft.
4) As a typical middle-class woman in the early 20th century, Sheila would have been expected to marry into money and be supported by her husband, rather than working herself.
5) Her parents are very pleased about her engagement — Gerald Croft is from an upper-class family, and his father is Mr Birling's main business competitor.
6) Their marriage will improve the Birlings' social standing, though it's implied that Gerald could have done better for himself socially.

> **Sheila Birling is...**
>
> childish: "Yes, go on, Mummy."
>
> empathetic: "I can't help thinking about this girl"
>
> honest: "But we really must stop these silly pretences."

Sheila can be immature and shallow...

1) Sheila admits to the Inspector in Act One that she got Eva/Daisy fired from Milwards as a childish reaction to being jealous of Eva/Daisy's looks and insecure about her own.
2) This means that an actor playing Sheila might want to emphasise her vanity and immaturity to ensure her confession is in keeping with her character, for example:

© Marilyn Kingwill / ArenaPAL

- Sheila is proud of her engagement ring — just after Gerald has given it to her, a performer could highlight this by gesturing exaggeratedly with the hand wearing the ring, as if trying to draw everyone else's attention to it.
- An actor playing Sheila could twirl their hair around their finger distractedly to show her youth and vanity.
- When Sheila calls Arthur and Sybil "Daddy" and "Mummy", an actor could use a soft, breathy voice to emphasise her immaturity.

... but she's also perceptive and compassionate

1) Sheila quickly understands what the Inspector is trying to do and sees where his questions are leading, e.g. she realises that the Inspector is trapping Mrs Birling into blaming Eric for Eva/Daisy's death at the end of Act Two.
2) She reveals that she thought there was something suspicious about Gerald's absence the previous summer, and she's not naive about life — she knows that some men use prostitutes and behave inappropriately, like Alderman Meggarty. She also reveals that she knows about Eric's drinking problem.
3) When Sheila confesses to getting Eva/Daisy fired, she says she "felt rotten about it at the time". This suggests that she already had a sense of compassion, even before the Inspector's questioning.

Character Performance — Sheila Birling

An actor's physicality should convey Sheila's character

1) Sheila is described as being young and *"rather excited"*.
2) Dynamic, lively movements could be used to convey Sheila's youth and excitement to the audience.
3) The actor playing Sheila could reflect her excitable nature by varying her intonation and pitch when delivering her lines.
4) Sheila's wealth and social status might give her a sense of confidence and entitlement, so an actor could use an upright posture or carefully poised gestures and movements to show this.

This actor uses elegant, poised gestures.
© Marilyn Kingwill / ArenaPAL

In Act One, Sheila becomes remorseful

1) When the play begins, Sheila comes across as relaxed and playful, but also naive and shallow.
2) When the Inspector questions her, she has a strong emotional reaction to what she did to Eva/Daisy and shows remorse and regret.

Act One — Physical Skills

- When Sheila speaks with *"mock aggressiveness"* to Gerald at the start of the act, she could lightly nudge his arm to show she's teasing him.
- When the Inspector reveals her part in Eva/Daisy's death, an actor playing Sheila could show her distress by wringing their hands or fidgeting with their clothes.

Act One — Vocal Skills

- When Sheila is answering the Inspector's questions and expressing remorse for her part in Eva/Daisy's death, an actor could lower the volume of their voice to create a grave tone.
- When Sheila explains how she behaved in Milwards, an actor could stutter and falter over her lines to show that her strong emotions are making it hard for her to speak.

Sheila tries to reason with her family in Act Two

1) In Act Two, Sheila is still distressed, but she's also aware of where the Inspector's questions are going.
2) She starts helping the Inspector by repeating his questions and asking her own, and tries to persuade her family and Gerald to co-operate — she wants them to be truthful and to stop trying to keep up pretences.
3) Sheila becomes more angry and assertive as the act goes on. She makes sarcastic remarks to Gerald when she learns about his affair with Eva/Daisy, and she refuses to be treated like a child by Mrs Birling.

Act Two — Physical Skills

- An actor might use closed body language to suggest that she's still ashamed, e.g. drawing her arms closer to her body or rounding her shoulders to seem smaller.
- Sheila's movements and gestures could become sudden and unpredictable as her frustration with her family grows.

Act Two — Vocal Skills

- When Mr Birling continues to resist the Inspector's questions and Sheila says "No, he's giving us rope — so that we'll hang ourselves", an actor could use an uneven tone of voice and disjointed phrasing to show her distress.
- An actor could use a cold tone of voice towards Gerald to show her disgust at his behaviour.

Character Performance — Sheila Birling

Sheila refuses to go back to her old self in Act Three

1) When the Inspector leaves in Act Three, Sheila <u>doesn't</u> get <u>excited</u> by the idea that the visit might have been a <u>hoax</u>. She realises that <u>regardless</u> of who Inspector Goole really was, his <u>message</u> is still important.

2) Sheila <u>doesn't</u> return to her <u>old ways</u> — her change is <u>permanent</u>. She's <u>shocked</u> that Mr and Mrs Birling and Gerald don't seem to have <u>learnt</u> anything from the Inspector's visit.

Effect on the Audience

When Sheila becomes <u>frustrated</u> with the others for not realising what they've done <u>wrong</u>, the audience are likely to feel <u>sympathy</u> towards her.

Act Three — Physical Skills

- An actor playing Sheila could place her <u>hands</u> on her <u>hips</u> and adopt a more <u>purposeful</u> <u>stance</u> to show how she has become <u>more assertive</u> with Gerald and her family.

- An actor could use <u>proxemics</u> to <u>convey</u> Sheila's different attitudes from her family, e.g. Sheila could <u>stand apart</u> from her parents to emphasise the <u>divide</u> between their views.

Act Three — Vocal Skills

- Sheila <u>mimics</u> Mr Birling when she says the line "<u>*That's all.*</u>" An actor playing her could <u>lower the pitch</u> of her <u>voice</u> and <u>copy</u> Mr Birling's <u>phrasing</u> in an <u>exaggerated</u> way to show that she is <u>mocking</u> him. Emphasising this line would show how she has <u>lost respect</u> for her father.

- At the <u>end</u> of the act, Sheila is <u>disturbed</u> by the other characters' <u>lack of compassion</u>. An actor could use a <u>strained</u> <u>tone of voice</u> to show her <u>shock</u> and <u>confusion</u>.

© Simon Gough Photography

Sheila's attitude to Gerald changes

1) Sheila's <u>relationship</u> with <u>Gerald</u> changes during the play, and this represents how her character <u>develops</u>.

2) <u>Before</u> the Inspector arrives, Sheila is already <u>suspicious</u> of Gerald's behaviour the previous summer by the way she teases him in a "*half serious, half playful*" way, however she's willing to <u>overlook</u> it because she's swept up in the <u>excitement</u> of her <u>engagement</u>.

3) When Sheila learns about Gerald's affair, she becomes <u>cynical</u>. An actor could use a <u>cold, detached tone</u> when she addresses Gerald and use <u>closed body language</u> such as <u>crossed arms</u> to show the <u>damage</u> he has done to their relationship.

4) When Gerald's questioning is <u>over</u>, Sheila gives her <u>engagement ring</u> back to him. This is the clearest evidence of Sheila's <u>change of attitude</u> — she's now prepared to <u>make her own decisions</u> and <u>challenge</u> her parents' wishes.

REVISION TASK

If only Sheila had done her clothes shopping online...

In a group, choose one person to be Sheila Birling and sit them in the 'hot seat'. Then take turns to question them — the person in the 'hot seat' must remain in character. You could ask:

1) How did the Inspector's questions make Sheila feel?
2) What would Sheila change about her past behaviour if she could?
3) What does Sheila think of Gerald now?

Imagine this interview is taking place at the end of Act Two.

Character Performance — Eric Birling

Like his sister, Eric Birling shows remorse for his part in Eva/Daisy's death. But he's not exactly a nice chap — he's got a lot to answer for. Take a look through these pages to get a sense of his complexity.

Eric is a troubled young man

1) Eric Birling is the <u>son</u> of Arthur and Sybil Birling, and the <u>brother</u> of Sheila.

2) He <u>drinks heavily</u> and spends <u>a lot of his time</u> at the Palace Bar, which is where he meets Eva/Daisy.

3) He's <u>uncomfortable</u> around his family — he <u>bickers</u> with his sister and seems to have a <u>tense relationship</u> with his parents.

Eric Birling is...

immature: *"You* told her. Why, you little sneak!"

awkward: "Suddenly I felt I just had to laugh."

troubled: "You don't understand anything. You never did. You never even tried — you —"

Effect on the Audience

The audience may feel <u>conflicted</u> about Eric. He's done some <u>terrible</u> things, but they may feel some <u>sympathy</u> towards him — his family <u>aren't supportive</u> and they <u>don't seem to respect him</u>.

He's got a lot of secrets

1) He's got a <u>drinking problem</u> — Gerald and Sheila know that he drinks quite a lot, but Mr and Mrs Birling <u>haven't got a clue</u>.

2) He was <u>drunk</u> when he met Eva/Daisy and it's implied that he <u>raped</u> her.

3) No one knows that he got Eva/Daisy <u>pregnant</u>. He tries to support her by <u>stealing money</u> from his father.

4) An actor playing Eric could behave <u>suspiciously</u> from the start of the play to hint that he's <u>hiding something</u>:

Side lighting and a worried expression make Eric look uneasy.

- He could <u>fiddle nervously</u> with <u>props</u> on the table to suggest he's <u>distracted</u> by something.

- <u>Avoiding eye contact</u> with the other characters or <u>darting his eyes</u> around the room could suggest Eric's <u>nervousness</u> and <u>guilt</u>.

- Eric's <u>shame</u> could be shown using a <u>hunched posture</u>.

He's used to heavy drinking

1) Eric is slightly <u>drunk</u> during the meal at the start of Act One. However, an actor would need to show this drunkenness <u>subtly</u>, as he's only "squiffy".

2) An actor playing Eric could use <u>slurred diction</u> or <u>raise the volume</u> of their <u>voice</u> to suggest this. They might also use <u>clumsy movements</u> and <u>gestures</u>.

3) By the end of the play, Eric seems to have <u>sobered up</u>. This might give the audience <u>hope</u> that he will <u>change</u> permanently.

Effect on the Audience

It's important for performers <u>not to overact</u> when pretending to be drunk — it can make a <u>serious</u> moment seem <u>comical</u> or <u>unrealistic</u>.

Character Performance — Eric Birling

Eric appears young and nervous

1) Eric is "*in his early twenties*" — director could cast an actor with a <u>slight build</u> to make Eric seem <u>younger</u> and <u>less physically imposing</u> on stage. An actor could also be <u>clean shaven</u> to suggest Eric's <u>youth</u>.

2) He is described as being "*not quite at ease*". A performer could use a <u>slouched posture</u> to make themselves seem <u>smaller</u> and more <u>awkward</u>.

3) Eric, Gerald and Mr Birling are all wearing "*tails and white ties*". The costume designer might want to reflect Eric's <u>unease</u> by making his suit <u>slightly looser</u> or <u>less well-fitting</u> than Gerald's.

Eric seems excitable and uneasy in Act One

1) He behaves <u>oddly</u> and <u>awkwardly</u> in Act One — e.g. he <u>laughs</u> for no apparent reason and cuts himself off <u>mid-sentence</u> without <u>explanation</u>.

2) His <u>relationship</u> with his <u>sister</u> in this act reveals his <u>immaturity</u> — they <u>bicker</u> with each other.

3) He comes across as the <u>least respected</u> member of the group — he's <u>interrupted</u> by his father and sister, and <u>told off</u> for his <u>behaviour</u> by his mother.

Act One — Physical Skills

- Eric could <u>roll his eyes</u> when he's <u>bickering</u> with Sheila. This would reflect his <u>immaturity</u>.
- When Eric is <u>interrupted</u>, an actor could show his <u>frustration</u> using <u>facial expressions</u>, e.g. <u>frowning</u> or <u>scowling</u>.
- An actor could <u>stumble</u> while they walk, or <u>drop props</u> on stage to help show that Eric is drunk. <u>Smiling</u> or attempting not to <u>laugh</u> at inappropriate moments would also help to convey his <u>drunkenness</u> to the audience.

Act One — Vocal Skills

- An actor playing Eric could <u>vary</u> the <u>volume</u>, <u>pitch</u> and <u>intonation</u> of his voice for <u>different</u> lines to reflect that he's "*half shy, half assertive*".
- Eric could use <u>pauses</u> before responding to the other characters to show his <u>lack of confidence</u>.
- An actor might <u>stress</u> the line "Women are potty about 'em" to suggest that Eric is trying to appear <u>mature</u> and <u>worldly</u> in front of Mr Birling and Gerald.

The audience doesn't see much of Eric in Act Two

1) Eric <u>isn't on stage</u> for most of Act Two — he only enters in the <u>final moment</u>, and doesn't have any lines.

2) The other characters do <u>talk about him</u> though. Sheila admits that he's had a <u>drinking problem</u> for <u>two years</u> and it is <u>revealed</u> that Eric was the <u>father</u> of Eva/Daisy's <u>unborn child</u>.

3) Eric finally rejoins the other characters "*looking <u>extremely pale</u> and <u>distressed</u>*". The stage directions also say that "*<u>he meets their inquiring stares</u>*".

Act Two — Physical Skills

- An actor might <u>walk</u> on stage <u>slowly</u>, using small, hesitant steps to convey Eric's <u>anxiety</u> and <u>fear</u> at having to <u>confront</u> the Inspector and <u>admit</u> to what he has done.
- To show his <u>nervousness</u> and <u>guilt</u>, he might also look <u>quickly</u> and <u>frantically</u> at each of the other characters on stage as they <u>stare back</u> at him <u>silently</u>.

© Vishal Sharma/Altrincham Garrick Playhouse

Character Performance — Eric Birling

Eric undergoes a big change in Act Three

1) Eric is questioned by the Inspector in Act Three — he becomes emotional and shows remorse for what he did to Eva/Daisy.

2) Eric also learns that Mrs Birling turned Eva/Daisy away from her charity. He blames his mother for Eva/Daisy's death and becomes angry and upset with her.

3) Eric changes by the end of the play — unlike his parents and Gerald, he isn't relieved when they think the Inspector was a trick. He takes responsibility for what he did, saying "You lot may be letting yourselves out nicely, but I can't."

©Vishal Sharma/Altrincham Garrick Playhouse

This production emphasised Eric's anger by having him lunge at Mrs Birling.

Act Three — Physical Skills

- Eric asks "*miserably*" if he can get a drink before he begins answering the Inspector's questions. He could hold a glass in front of him and focus on it sadly to remind the audience of the part alcohol played when he met Eva/Daisy.
- When Mr Birling asks where Eric got the fifty pounds from, Eric "*does not reply*". A performer could emphasise this silence by hanging his head to suggest his guilt.
- He might shake Mrs Birling violently by the shoulders when he realises she refused to help Eva/Daisy. This aggressive behaviour would show his anger and lack of control.

Act Three — Vocal Skills

- When Eric is trying to persuade his parents that the Inspector's message was important, he could speak more slowly and with a deeper pitch to reinforce how seriously he is taking the Inspector's message. A deeper voice could also suggest how Eric has matured as a character.
- When Eric says to his father "What does it matter now whether they give you a knighthood or not?", an actor could spit out this line angrily to show his contempt.

In the exam, link performance suggestions to the text

Have a look at this sample answer — it has some ideas about how you could write about Eric.

This shows a clear focus on a specific moment.

> When Eric says "You know, don't you?" at the start of Act Three, I would use a higher pitch and strained tone of voice to show that he is nervous and distressed. When the Inspector replies "Yes, we know", I would react by sagging my shoulders and dropping my gaze to avoid making eye contact with any of the other characters. Using body language in this way would suggest that Eric is resigned and ashamed. When he "comes farther in", I would stand in the centre of all the characters. Being surrounded by other characters would suggest that Eric is trapped.

This links the performance to the text by demonstrating a reaction to the Inspector's line.

This shows how characterisation is supported by aspects of performance.

This further develops the point.

EXAM TIP

Yet another delightful member of the Birling family...

Eric is a miserable figure, but his actions mean that the audience are likely to have a mixed reaction to him — consider how an actor might communicate his complexity to the audience through their performance.

Character Performance — Gerald Croft

Gerald Croft is confident, charming and upper class. Don't be fooled though — he had a part in the fate of Eva/Daisy like everyone else. Read on for some ideas on how he could be presented on stage...

Gerald is Sheila's fiancé

1) Gerald is <u>engaged</u> to Sheila Birling — he's at the Birlings' house to <u>celebrate</u> their engagement.

2) He's the Birlings' <u>social superior</u> — he's a member of the <u>upper class</u>. His mother is Lady Croft and his father is Sir George Croft, whose business is <u>larger</u> and <u>older</u> than Mr Birling's.

3) Gerald had an <u>affair</u> with Eva Smith and kept her as a <u>mistress</u> — though he knew her as <u>Daisy Renton</u>.

Effect on the Audience

Gerald could be performed in <u>several</u> ways. He treated Eva/Daisy with <u>kindness</u>, so a performer could emphasise his <u>sympathetic qualities</u>. However, he <u>doesn't learn</u> from the Inspector's visit, so an actor may want to portray him as <u>cold</u> instead.

Gerald Croft is...

confident: "Getting a bit heavy-handed, aren't you, Inspector?"
a liar: "I wasn't telling you a complete lie"
charitable: "I didn't ask for anything in return."

He's an upper-class man of about thirty

1) The stage directions describe Gerald as "*an <u>attractive chap</u> about <u>thirty</u>*".

2) A director might cast a tall actor with a <u>strong build</u> to reflect that he is "*rather <u>too manly</u> to be a dandy*". Casting a <u>taller</u> actor could also give the impression that Gerald is <u>confident</u>.

> A 'dandy' was a man who placed a lot of importance on dressing fashionably and leading a leisurely lifestyle.

3) An actor could wear <u>shoes with a taller heel</u> to make him loom over <u>Mr Birling</u>. The difference in <u>height</u> could <u>remind</u> the audience of their <u>difference in class</u>.

4) Gerald is also described as being "*<u>well-bred</u>*" — an actor could use an <u>upright posture</u> and <u>stick out his chest</u> to suggest a sense of <u>entitlement</u>.

Effect on the Audience

Gerald's <u>easy confidence</u> could make Eric's <u>awkwardness</u> seem more <u>prominent</u> to an audience.

In Act One, Gerald is confident and charming

1) At the start of Act One, Gerald is <u>affectionate</u> with Sheila. He's also <u>warm</u>, <u>easy-going</u> and <u>familiar</u> with the rest of the Birlings.

2) At the end of the act, Gerald is "*<u>startled</u>*" when the Inspector says that Eva Smith <u>changed</u> her name to Daisy Renton. Sheila immediately becomes <u>suspicious</u>, and Gerald <u>admits</u> that he had an <u>affair</u> with her.

© Simon Gough Photography

Act One — Vocal Skills

- An actor could use <u>Received Pronunciation</u> to show Gerald's <u>higher social class</u>.

- An actor could <u>lower the volume</u> of his <u>voice</u> when saying "<u>I drink to you</u>" to make the moment between Sheila and Gerald more <u>intimate</u> and <u>affectionate</u>.

Act One — Physical Skills

- <u>Smiling</u> and making direct <u>eye contact</u> with the other characters could show Gerald's <u>confident</u>, <u>easy-going</u> nature.

- When Gerald hears Daisy Renton's name, an actor might <u>stand up</u> quickly or <u>step backwards</u> suddenly to show his <u>surprise</u>. An actor could reinforce this shock by pouring himself a <u>drink</u>.

Character Performance — Gerald Croft

In Act Two, he's honest with the Inspector

1) Gerald is <u>honest</u> when questioned by the Inspector in Act Two. He expresses <u>remorse</u> about what happened to Eva/Daisy, but he seems to <u>repress</u> his <u>emotions</u> — he is <u>suddenly</u> hit by her death and asks for some time alone.

2) The <u>revelations</u> about his affair with Eva/Daisy <u>damage</u> his relationship with Sheila. She gives the <u>engagement ring</u> back to Gerald.

A furrowed brow and downcast eyes suggest that Gerald feels remorseful.

© Vishal Sharma/Altrincham Garrick Playhouse

Act Two — Physical Skills

- An actor might <u>sit very still</u> as he describes his affair with Eva/Daisy to suggest that he's <u>trying hard</u> to keep his emotions <u>under control</u>.
- As the questioning continues, Gerald's <u>posture</u> could <u>gradually</u> become <u>hunched</u> to show that he feels <u>guilt</u> for how he treated Eva/Daisy.

Act Two — Vocal Skills

- Gerald keeps his <u>outward emotions</u> in <u>control</u> during most of the Inspector's questioning. An actor could keep his voice <u>level</u> and <u>calm</u> to reflect this. An actor could use <u>natural phrasing</u> to show that Gerald thinks <u>logically</u> and <u>carefully</u> and does not react impulsively.
- However, Gerald seems <u>distressed</u> when he says "I'm rather more — <u>upset</u> [...] than I probably <u>appear</u> to be." An actor could <u>reflect</u> this by <u>breathing heavily</u> between words.
- When Gerald exits, he says "But I'm coming back — if I may." This line could be spoken <u>hesitantly</u> to Sheila and with a <u>rising inflection</u>, to show that he is <u>asking</u> her for <u>permission</u>.

He hasn't really changed by the end of Act Three

1) When Gerald <u>returns</u> to the house, he's <u>excited</u> to reveal that the Inspector wasn't a real police officer.

2) He isn't <u>changed</u> by the Inspector's visit. Like Mr and Mrs Birling, he's <u>relieved</u> and <u>triumphant</u> at the idea that the Inspector might have been a <u>hoax</u>.

Act Three — Vocal Skills

- Gerald "*slowly*" reveals that the Inspector wasn't a real police officer. An actor could speak his next lines at a <u>much quicker pace</u> to <u>contrast</u> with this and show his <u>excitement</u>.
- An actor could reflect Gerald's <u>relief</u> by using a <u>bright tone</u> and a <u>bouncy rhythm</u>.

Act Three — Physical Skills

- Gerald's relief could be shown through <u>relaxed body language</u> — he might <u>flop into a chair</u> and put his <u>hands behind</u> his <u>head</u>.
- Gerald could put his <u>arm around Sheila affectionately</u> when he says "What about this ring?" to show that he wants their <u>relationship</u> to <u>be like before</u>, as if <u>nothing</u> has happened.

REVISION TASK

Gerald's posher than a top hat full of caviar...

Choose a moment from Act Two featuring Gerald. In a group, act out this moment without using any words. Try to communicate the scene's meaning using physical skills, for instance:

1) Facial expressions and eye contact.
2) Gestures and body language.
3) The use of proxemics to convey relationships on stage.

> If you're revising by yourself, try writing a couple of paragraphs about how you would do this.

Character Performance — Eva/Daisy

Although she doesn't have any lines, Eva/Daisy's death is the reason the Inspector calls in the first place. There wouldn't be a play without her, so make sure you understand what she represents...

Eva/Daisy's death drives the whole plot

1) She's known both as <u>Eva Smith</u> and <u>Daisy Renton</u>. She is a <u>young</u>, <u>pretty</u>, <u>working-class woman</u> who has no family of her own.

2) Eva/Daisy <u>commits suicide</u> by drinking disinfectant. During the play, the Inspector <u>questions</u> each of the characters and reveals how they <u>all contributed</u> to her fate.

3) The Inspector uses his <u>questions</u> about Eva/Daisy's <u>life</u> and <u>death</u> to make the Birlings <u>examine</u> their <u>own behaviour</u>.

> **Eva/Daisy is...**
>
> **principled:** "She'd had a lot to say — far too much"
> **moral:** "she didn't want to take the stolen money?"
> **vulnerable:** "She was here alone, friendless, almost penniless, desperate."

She could appear on stage in non-naturalistic productions

1) In Priestley's <u>script</u>, Eva/Daisy <u>doesn't</u> appear <u>on stage</u>, but a director may choose to include her in the <u>performance</u>.

2) A <u>director</u> could show her using <u>shadow theatre</u>, <u>film reels</u> or <u>puppets</u>. For example, a <u>film reel</u> might be <u>projected</u> onto a screen or backdrop to show Eva/Daisy lying in the <u>morgue</u>. Showing this on stage would make her death even more <u>shocking</u> for the audience.

> Showing Eva/Daisy on stage through flashbacks or as a ghost would make a performance non-naturalistic, and would remind the audience they're watching a play.

3) Eva/Daisy could also be portrayed by an <u>actor</u>. A director might use the role in <u>different ways</u>:

- An actor could be positioned <u>on stage</u> but remain <u>silent</u> and '<u>unseen</u>' by the other characters. Eva/Daisy could stand with her <u>shoulders rounded</u> or <u>widen her eyes</u> to highlight her <u>innocence</u> and <u>vulnerability</u>. She could use <u>movements</u> to <u>react</u> to the characters' <u>dialogue</u> to hint at her character's emotions, e.g. when it's <u>revealed</u> that she was <u>pregnant</u>, an actor could <u>caress her stomach</u> lovingly.

- An actor could be used in <u>flashbacks</u>, e.g. when Mr Birling talks about Eva/Daisy <u>striking</u> at the factory, an actor could <u>hold</u> a <u>sign</u> saying '<u>Fair pay for all</u>'. An actor could be positioned on a <u>different level</u> to suggest that she's representing events that happened in the <u>past</u>.

- In his <u>final speech</u>, the Inspector says there are "<u>millions of Eva Smiths</u>". This reinforces the idea that Eva/Daisy represents <u>working-class women</u> everywhere. A <u>different actor</u> could be used for each part of her <u>story</u> throughout the play to <u>emphasise</u> the idea that her <u>fate</u> could have happened to <u>anyone</u> in her <u>situation</u>.

Effect on the Audience

Showing Eva/Daisy <u>on stage</u> might make her seem <u>more real</u> to the audience. Being able to see her <u>reactions</u> to the Birlings could create <u>sympathy</u> for her.

Effect on the Audience

By the <u>end</u>, it <u>isn't clear</u> whether there was <u>one woman</u> called Eva who went by <u>other names</u>, or if the Birlings met several <u>different people</u>. This may leave the audience feeling <u>confused</u> or <u>unsettled</u>.

Spoiler alert — this play does not end happily Eva after...

If Eva/Daisy appears on stage, she creates some unique challenges for the actor playing her. The fact that she doesn't have any lines means that physical performance is really important.

Character Performance — Edna

Edna, the Birlings' parlourmaid, may not have a huge amount to say or do during the course of the play, but her character still brings something important to the table (and not just the Birlings' dinner).

Edna is employed by the Birlings

1) Edna is a <u>working-class woman</u> employed by the Birlings as a <u>maid</u>.

2) Edna's <u>presence</u> on stage <u>reminds</u> the audience of the Birlings' <u>wealth</u> and <u>status</u>.

3) Priestley doesn't give much information about her <u>character</u> or <u>appearance</u> in the stage directions, so it's up to the director to decide how to <u>portray</u> her.

Edna is...

dutiful: "Edna'll go. I asked her to wait up to make us some tea."

silent: "Giving us the port, Edna? That's right."

obedient: "Yes, ma'am."

She's obedient and dutiful

The Birlings are Edna's <u>employers</u> and her <u>social superiors</u>, so an actor might use <u>physical skills</u> to show her <u>respect</u> and <u>obedience</u>:

- <u>Curtseying</u> and <u>nodding</u> could show that she's <u>obedient</u>.
- An actor could keep her <u>head bowed</u> in the presence of the family to show her <u>respect</u> for their <u>higher social status</u>.

Effect on the Audience

A <u>director</u> may want the actors playing the Birlings and Gerald to treat Edna <u>dismissively</u> or to largely <u>ignore</u> her. This would create <u>sympathy</u> for Edna and present the Birlings and Gerald as <u>disrespectful</u>.

She represents the working class

1) Edna is usually the only <u>working-class</u> character on stage.

2) An actor could use a <u>strong regional accent</u> to show that Edna is from a <u>different background</u> to the Birlings.

3) She could be played by an <u>old</u> or <u>young</u> actor. An older actor could move <u>gingerly</u> and <u>frailly</u> across the stage in order to highlight the <u>hardships</u> of life for <u>working-class</u> people and help to create a feeling of <u>sympathy</u> in the audience.

4) Casting a <u>young actor</u> in this role might be <u>effective</u> as she could be a <u>visual reminder</u> of Eva/Daisy and the <u>struggles</u> she faced. A young actor playing Edna could move <u>clumsily</u>, which could attract <u>disapproving looks</u> from the Birlings. This would help to <u>link</u> her to the way the Birlings treated <u>Eva/Daisy</u>.

© Vishal Sharma/Altrincham Garrick Playhouse

REVISION TASK

Rumour has it that Edna's actually a right chatterbox...

Imagine that Edna has been listening at the door during Act One. Write a soliloquy for Edna to deliver to the audience between Acts One and Two revealing her thoughts on what she's heard. You should think about:

1) How the language you choose could reflect Edna's working-class background.

2) The way Edna could use her physical and vocal performance skills to support her performance.

Tick list:

✓ language choice

✓ appropriate physical and vocal performance skills

✓ audience interaction

Practice Questions

What an absolute bunch of characters — and you should hopefully have some pretty good ideas about how to perform each of them by now. Have a go at these practice questions to test what you've learnt...

Quick Questions

1) What type of build might an actor playing the Inspector have? Explain why.

2) Give one feature that makes the Inspector seem intimidating to the other characters.

3) Give one reason why Mr Birling seems selfish in Act One.

4) What is Arthur Birling insecure about?

5) Why does Sybil Birling become distressed at the end of Act Two?

6) Find three quotes from the text that show Sheila is changed by the Inspector.

7) Give one aspect of Eric's backstory that contributes to how he behaves in the play.

8) Why does Gerald become triumphant and excited when he returns in Act Three?

9) What group of people might Eva/Daisy be intended to represent?

10) How could an actor playing Edna show her obedience to the Birlings?

In-depth Questions

1) How might an actor playing the Inspector use physical performance skills to seem purposeful?

2) How might an actor playing Mr Birling use vocal skills to show how he feels in control at the start of Act One?

3) How could an actor playing Sybil express her dislike for the Inspector in Act Two?

4) How does Sheila change over the course of the play? Explain how this could be reflected in performance.

5) Explain how an actor might use performance skills to communicate Eric's drunkenness.

6) If Eva/Daisy were to be physically portrayed on stage, suggest three ways in which a director could choose to do this.

Practice Questions

Itching for some exam-style practice? Well, it's your lucky day. Here are five questions to get you thinking about performance skills. Don't just have a go at the easiest questions — make sure you tackle them all. That way you'll be better prepared for whatever the exam throws at you.

Exam-style Questions

> Find the part of Act Two where Gerald is telling the Inspector about how he knew Eva/Daisy. Read from where the Inspector says "**I see.**" up to "***She hands him the ring.***", then answer Questions 1 and 2 below.

1) Imagine you're playing the Inspector. He is an authoritative character in the play. Explain how you would use performance skills to show his authority in this extract, giving reasons for your ideas.

2) Imagine you're playing Sheila. Her relationship with Gerald deteriorates during the play. Explain how you would use performance skills to communicate this to the audience during the extract, giving reasons for your ideas.

> Find the part of Act Two where the Inspector questions Mrs Birling. Read from where the Inspector "***turns to Mrs Birling***" to where Mrs Birling says "**I've done nothing wrong — and you know it**", then answer Question 3.

3) Imagine you're directing a production of *An Inspector Calls*. Explain how a performer playing the character of Mrs Birling might demonstrate to the audience her self-confidence in this extract and elsewhere in the play. You should talk about performance skills, stage directions and use of stage space in your answer.

> Find the part of Act Three where Eric is questioned by the Inspector. Read from where the Inspector says "**When did you meet her again?**" to where Eric says "**You never even tried — you —**", then answer Questions 4 and 5 below.

4) Imagine you're directing a production of *An Inspector Calls*. Explain how a performer playing the character of Eric might demonstrate to the audience his distress and guilt in this extract and elsewhere in the play. You should talk about performance skills, stage directions and use of stage space in your answer.

5) Imagine you're directing a production of *An Inspector Calls*. Explain how a performer playing the character of Birling might demonstrate to the audience his strained relationship with Eric in this extract and elsewhere in the play. You should talk about performance skills, stage directions and use of stage space in your answer.

Stage Types and Stage Design

It's usually the director who chooses the stage type and decides how the production should look. Directors need to make sure that their choices are appropriate for the style of the production.

The stage type needs to work for the whole play

1) A director should choose a stage type to <u>suit</u> the <u>style</u> of their production.

2) *An Inspector Calls* was written to be <u>staged</u> and <u>performed</u> in a <u>naturalistic style</u> (see p. 22). In naturalistic productions, the stage is often <u>set back</u> from the audience, which helps to maintain the 'fourth wall' (see p. 22). This adds to the illusion that the audience is observing <u>real life</u> playing out on stage.

3) Priestley suggests that the play should use a <u>proscenium arch stage</u> — he refers to the "*rise*" of a "*curtain*" in the stage directions. This helps to keep the sense that the play is real life — viewing the play through the <u>arch</u> can help the audience to imagine that they're looking into the Birlings' dining room.

4) <u>Non-naturalistic productions</u> (see p. 22) might use a stage type that brings the actors <u>closer</u> to the audience. This might make it easier for them to <u>break the fourth wall</u>, which would remind the audience that they are watching a play.

5) The director also needs to think about the <u>practicalities</u> of each <u>stage type.</u> This could include how the stage type <u>affects</u> the <u>positioning of scenery and furniture</u>, how actors <u>enter</u> and <u>exit</u> the stage, as well as the audience's <u>sightlines</u> (their view of the action on stage).

A proscenium arch stage.

© Donald Cooper/ photostage

Different stage types create different effects

1) **Proscenium arch** and **end-on staging** allow directors to use <u>backdrops</u> and large pieces of <u>scenery</u> without affecting the audience's <u>sightlines</u>. Since the action of *An Inspector Calls* only takes place in <u>one</u> setting, a director can use <u>detailed</u> scenery and stage furniture without having to worry about <u>transitions</u> between acts. Detailed scenery can also add to the play's <u>realism</u>.

Using end-on staging allowed this production to use a detailed set.

© Vishal Sharma/Altrincham Garrick Playhouse

2) A <u>disadvantage</u> of these stage types is that it's <u>harder</u> for audience members who are sitting further back to <u>see</u> the actors' <u>facial expressions clearly</u>. This could <u>reduce the emotional impact</u> of key moments, for example, when Sybil realises that Eva/Daisy was pregnant with Sybil's grandchild.

3) **Traverse staging**, where audience members are sitting <u>opposite each other</u>, can make the action feel <u>less realistic</u>, because it reminds them that they are <u>watching a play</u>. However, this stage type could be used to reinforce the play's idea that we are all <u>responsible</u> for each other in society.

4) **Theatre in the round**, where audience members are seated on <u>all sides</u> of a central stage, can create a <u>claustrophobic</u> atmosphere, which could show how the Birlings are <u>trapped</u> and cannot escape the <u>consequences</u> of their actions. It could also create the sense that the family is being <u>examined</u> and <u>judged</u> from all sides with nowhere left for them to hide.

5) **Thrust staging**, where audience members are sitting on three sides of the stage, can create an <u>intimate atmosphere</u>. Staging <u>key emotional scenes</u>, for example the Inspector's final speech in Act Three, on the <u>apron</u> would <u>involve the audience</u> more closely in the scene.

6) **Site-specific theatre** could be used <u>effectively</u> in *An Inspector Calls* — staging the play in the dining room of a country house could help to <u>immerse</u> the audience in the story.

Stage Types and Stage Design

Staging and performance space are linked

1) Directors need to think about how to use space on stage.

2) A director could choose a small performance space to reinforce the play's claustrophobic atmosphere (p. 23).

3) A larger space would make blocking easier. This would help make the actions and reactions of each character clearly visible to the audience members.

4) A director should also consider how different areas of the stage might be used effectively. Stages are often split into nine areas.

5) Stage areas are important when positioning actors. For example, in Act Three, Sheila and Eric could be positioned downstage right whereas Mr and Mrs Birling and Gerald could be standing upstage left. The proxemics would visually represent the growing distance between the characters' views.

Upstage Right (USR)	Upstage Centre (USC)	Upstage Left (USL)
Stage Right (SR)	Centre Stage (CS)	Stage Left (SL)
Downstage Right (DSR)	Downstage Centre (DSC)	Downstage Left (DSL)

AUDIENCE

When the audience is sitting on more than one side of the stage, one part of the stage is picked as 'downstage', and this is used as a reference for the other terms.

Stage type affects entrance and exit points

1) Priestley's stage directions mention characters entering and exiting through a door to the dining room — at the end of Act One "*The door slowly opens and the* Inspector *appears*".

2) Priestley doesn't specify where this door should be, so its position needs to be decided by the director.

3) If the play is staged on a proscenium arch stage, a director may choose to incorporate the door upstage centre to focus the audience's attention on the Inspector's arrival in Act One.

4) A director may choose to have more than one entrance / exit point. However, in a naturalistic production, entrance and exit points would be restricted by the play's setting — a realistic dining room would only have a couple of doors.

5) A non-naturalistic production could use exits and entrances to reinforce the Inspector's supernatural characteristics. At the end of Act One, the Inspector may appear silently from the side of the stage, without using a door, while the audience's attention is focused on Sheila and Gerald.

6) Characters could also enter and exit through the aisles between the audience. Directing the Inspector to appear in the walkways as he makes his entrance in Act One would create the same feeling of surprise in the audience that is experienced by the characters on stage, reinforcing the unsettling feeling created by his arrival.

This production incorporated a working door into the set.

© Vishal Sharma/Altrincham Garrick Playhouse

REVISION TASK

The thrust stage was mad when I broke its fourth wall...

Imagine that you are staging the play on a thrust stage. Draw a sketch that shows where you would position the entrance and exit points. Make sure you think about:

1) The style of the production (i.e. naturalistic, non-naturalistic).
2) What the audience would and would not be able to see.
3) The dramatic effects your design would create.

Tick list:
✓ specific design details
✓ limitations of stage types
✓ the effect on the audience

Set Design

Set design is really important — it's vital for establishing the play's setting, context and style.

Set design should support the style of the production

1) Priestley provides <u>instructions</u> for the set design in the <u>stage directions</u>. He describes the play as taking place in a "*dining-room of a fairly large suburban house*" and having a "*substantial and heavily comfortable, but not cosy and homelike*" <u>atmosphere</u>.

2) A director can <u>choose</u> to ignore the playwright's suggestions for set design. Priestley acknowledges that his ideas <u>may not work</u> for every production, and he suggests that some productions may wish to "*dispense with an ordinary realistic set*". No matter what a director chooses, it's important that it <u>suits the style</u> of the production.

3) A <u>naturalistic</u> production might use a <u>historically accurate</u> set to recreate an <u>early 20th-century</u>, <u>middle-class home</u>. This would add to the illusion that the events the audience is watching are <u>real</u>.

4) A <u>non-naturalistic</u> production may use set design to <u>highlight</u> the <u>themes</u> of the play. For example, a <u>silhouette</u> of a large pair of <u>unbalanced scales</u> could be printed on the backdrop. This could be used to represent the <u>unfair distribution</u> of wealth and power in early 20th-century society.

The details of a set design can reinforce the setting...

A naturalistic design might use <u>authentic materials</u> and <u>colours</u> to make the play's setting seem more <u>realistic</u>.

MATERIALS

1) In the 1910s, rooms which were <u>ornate</u> and <u>highly decorative</u> were a sign of <u>wealth</u>. A designer could show the Birlings' <u>social position</u> by using elegant wallpaper in the dining room.

2) <u>Plastic</u> wasn't widely used until the 1940s, so a naturalistic set would try to <u>avoid</u> <u>plastics</u> and <u>synthetic materials</u> in favour of <u>natural</u> materials, like <u>wood</u> and <u>leather</u>.

3) The stage directions mention a <u>fireplace</u> — fireplaces at the turn of the century were often made from <u>cast iron</u>. Cast iron is very <u>heavy</u>, so a set designer may want to use a more <u>practical</u> material, such as polystyrene, and paint it to look <u>authentic</u>.

4) <u>Soft furnishings</u>, such as curtains, might be made from thick fabrics, like <u>velvet</u>.

COLOURS

1) <u>Deeper colours</u> for walls and fabrics were popular at the time the play is set, so choosing a <u>similar colour palette</u> would add to the <u>realism</u>.

2) <u>Bright</u>, <u>chemically enhanced</u> colours, such as hot pink or lime green, would look out of place, so they should be <u>avoided</u> in a naturalistic set.

Set Designers

It's important that set designers consider the <u>practicalities</u> of their set. Some materials might be <u>expensive</u> or <u>heavy</u>, so it's the designer's responsibility to find <u>alternatives</u> that still <u>suit</u> the style of the production.

... and they can also create symbolism

1) Designers can use aspects of the set, e.g. the <u>colours</u>, to symbolise the <u>themes</u> and <u>messages</u> of the play.

2) Using a <u>deep</u>, <u>dark red</u> for the furnishings of the Birlings' home could suggest <u>danger</u>, <u>death</u> and <u>blood</u> to the audience. This could symbolise how the upper classes <u>benefit</u> from the <u>exploitation</u> of the lower classes.

3) Having <u>dark curtains</u> gradually move in from the side of the stage could symbolise how Eva/Daisy's death is starting to <u>intrude</u> on the Birlings' <u>privileged lives</u>.

Colour Symbolism

Colour symbolism uses the <u>feelings</u> and <u>ideas</u> that are associated with certain <u>colours</u> to create <u>meaning</u> for the audience.

Set Design

Levels can show character relationships or themes

Priestley's <u>stage directions</u> don't describe <u>levels</u>, but a designer could still include them in their <u>set design</u>.

1) Levels can be used to <u>highlight key moments</u>. For example, when the Inspector shows Sheila the photograph in Act One, the characters could be stood on a <u>rostrum</u> (raised platform).

2) Levels could be used to <u>reinforce characters' personalities</u>. When Mrs Birling first enters in Act Two, she could come down a set of <u>stairs</u> to emphasise how she feels <u>above</u> other people.

3) Levels can also show <u>relationships</u> between characters. Positioning the men on a <u>lower level</u> when the Inspector makes his first entrance could highlight how the Inspector <u>takes control</u> of the situation.

4) A director can use levels to show <u>character development</u>. A <u>sloping stage</u> could be used to show the <u>difference in morals</u> between the Inspector and the Birlings. As the play progresses, Sheila and Eric could gradually <u>move up the stage</u> towards the Inspector, suggesting that they want to <u>change</u> and <u>learn</u> from the Inspector's warnings.

© Alastair Muir/REX/Shutterstock

5) Levels can help to emphasise the play's <u>themes</u>. The stage could be positioned <u>lower than the audience</u>, so that the audience <u>looks down</u> on the action. This would <u>align</u> the audience with the <u>Inspector</u> and encourage the idea that they are meant to <u>judge</u> the Birlings and their actions.

Technical features support the action on stage

Set designers need to make sure that any special effects fit in with the overall style of the production.

1) Technical features can make performances run <u>more smoothly</u>. Priestley suggests using a <u>revolving stage</u> to move the dining table after Act One. This creates <u>more space</u> on stage for the characters to move around, and allows the scene to <u>transition</u> without the <u>interruption</u> of stagehands.

2) Technical features can also be used to create <u>special effects</u> on stage:

Technical Device	Potential use in *An Inspector Calls*	Dramatic Effect
Projectors	A <u>window</u> looking onto the street could be projected onto the scenery, initially showing a light evening which <u>gradually changes</u> into a <u>dark, stormy night</u>.	This would help to show the <u>progression of time</u> as the play unfolds. The changing weather would emphasise the <u>mood</u> on stage, with the storm reflecting the <u>sinister nature</u> of the night's revelations.
Smoke machines	Smoke machines could release a <u>light mist</u> onto the stage as the Inspector enters in Act One.	The mist would reinforce the Inspector's <u>supernatural nature</u> as well as <u>creating tension</u> for the audience by <u>masking</u> his entrance.
Pyrotechnics	Pyrotechnics could be used to create a <u>fire</u> in the fireplace. The fire could <u>flare up</u> briefly when the Inspector says "they will be taught it in fire and blood and anguish".	Having a <u>real fire</u> would make the setting feel more <u>realistic</u>. Making the fire flare up during the Inspector's closing speech would highlight the <u>intensity</u> of his words.
Film reels	In a <u>non-naturalistic</u> production, a <u>video flashback</u> of each character's treatment of Eva/Daisy could be <u>projected</u> onto the backdrop as they confess.	Showing a visual flashback could make the performance more <u>engaging</u>. It could also encourage an <u>emotional response</u> from the audience as they can witness <u>first-hand</u> how <u>unjustly</u> she was treated.

Set Design

Set design adds to the overall impact of the play

1) Each part of the set needs to <u>complement</u> the style of the production — a naturalistic set design that included non-naturalistic features could have a <u>jarring effect</u> on the audience.

2) Set designers also need to think about <u>atmosphere</u>. The overall atmosphere of the play is <u>tense</u> — the designer could make the setting of the dining room <u>tall and imposing</u>, with little space within the room, in order to emphasise the feeling of <u>tension</u> and <u>claustrophobia</u> felt by the characters.

3) Non-naturalistic set designs can be used to emphasise a particular <u>theme</u> or <u>idea</u>, adding to the play's impact and message. A designer could choose to acknowledge the <u>context</u> in which the play was written (Britain in the 1940s) by setting the play in an <u>air-raid shelter</u>.

4) If a director wanted to emphasise the theme of <u>class inequality</u>, they could stage the dining room on a <u>raised level</u> above a <u>cramped factory floor</u> filled with workers. This would emphasise the <u>exploitation</u> of the working class.

© Alastair Muir/REX/Shutterstock

5) Stephen Daldry's production of *An Inspector Calls* (see p. 22) created a set in the style of an <u>Edwardian doll's house</u>. The doll's house eventually comes crashing down, which reflects how the characters' lives have been <u>disrupted</u> by the Inspector.

Include specific details about set design in exam answers

In the exam, it's important to include <u>specific details</u> when you're talking about the <u>overall effect</u> that you're trying to create through set design. Here's an example of how you could write about the <u>design of a setting</u>:

> It's important the set design matches the <u>style</u> of the production.

For a non-naturalistic production of the play, I would include a room in Eva/Daisy's home on one side of the stage, which would be much smaller and more run-down than the Birlings' dining room.

> This explains the <u>overall effect</u> that you want to achieve.

I would use polystyrene blocks painted to look like grey stone for the walls, cracked plastic in the windows to represent broken glass, and peeling brown wallpaper to show the state of disrepair.

> This gives <u>precise details</u> about <u>materials</u> and <u>colours</u>.

This would make it seem like an uncomfortable place to live. The split set would reflect the contrast in quality of life for lower and middle/upper-class people in 1912, and encourage the audience to feel sympathy for Eva/Daisy.

> This considers the <u>symbolic</u> effect of the set.

REVISION TASK

A joke told in a lift works on so many levels...

Imagine you are staging a naturalistic production of 'An Inspector Calls'. Write a brief paragraph that describes the set design and scenery you'd use for the Birlings' dining room. Think about:

1) The materials, textures and colours you'd use.
2) The overall atmosphere you're trying to create.
3) Why your choices are suitable for a naturalistic production of *An Inspector Calls*.

Tick list:
- ✓ specific design details
- ✓ how historical context can influence design choices
- ✓ the effect on the audience

Props and Stage Furniture

Props and stage furniture aren't just for decoration — they help the audience understand key details of the play.

Props and stage furniture can communicate setting...

1) In a <u>naturalistic production</u>, a set designer would choose props and stage furniture that show the setting of a <u>middle-class home</u> at the <u>start of the 20th century</u>. For example, the use of electricity wasn't widespread at this time, so <u>replica gas lamps</u> would help to convey this time period.

2) <u>Expensive</u>, <u>ornate</u> furniture such as <u>carved wooden chairs</u> with <u>velvet seat pads</u> could suggest the Birlings' <u>wealth</u> to the audience.

3) Priestley refers to various props and furniture in his <u>stage directions</u> — at the start of Act One, "*champagne glasses*" should be on the table. These props help to establish the <u>after-dinner setting</u>. Using champagne glasses also reinforces the <u>celebratory atmosphere</u>, as well as hinting at the Birlings' <u>extravagant lifestyle</u>.

4) Stage furniture can also communicate the <u>time of day</u>. In Act One, the Inspector "*moves nearer a light — perhaps standard lamp*" to show the photograph to Sheila. Using <u>lit lamps</u> would suggest that the action is taking place in the <u>evening</u>.

©Vishal Sharma/Altrincham Garrick Playhouse

This naturalistic production of 'An Inspector Calls' uses historically accurate props and stage furniture.

... or help to drive the action

1) Some of the props are <u>pivotal to the plot</u>. For example, the Inspector's <u>photo</u> of Eva/Daisy is used to <u>extract confessions</u> from the characters.

2) The telephone in Act Three is also <u>crucial</u> — it <u>enables the twist</u> at the end of the play.

Set Design

The phone could be placed <u>downstage</u> and the performers on stage could be directed to <u>gather</u> around it when Birling answers the call. This would signal to the audience that the phone call is <u>significant</u>, and the family standing together in <u>shocked silence</u> would be a memorable <u>final moment</u> as the curtain falls.

Personal props can reinforce characterisation

A <u>personal prop</u> is a prop that is used by an actor to add <u>depth</u> to their character.

1) Sheila's obsession with her <u>ring</u> in Act One shows her <u>naivety</u> — she's <u>excited</u> about the engagement even though she is <u>suspicious</u> about Gerald's behaviour. Sheila gives Gerald the ring back when she finds out about his past — this shows how much the Inspector's visit has <u>changed</u> her.

2) The actor who plays Eric could consistently <u>hold</u> and <u>refill</u> a <u>whisky glass</u> to hint at his "*familiarity with quick heavy drinking*".

Props

Props can also have <u>symbolic meaning</u>, for example any <u>decanters and bottles of alcohol</u> on stage could symbolise the Birlings' <u>wealth</u> and <u>social status</u>. When the Inspector arrives in Act One, Birling offers him a drink, which suggests that Birling is accustomed to using his <u>wealth</u> and <u>position</u> to <u>influence</u> others. The Inspector's <u>refusal</u> of the drink suggests that he <u>won't</u> be swayed by Birling's power.

EXAM TIP

The content of this page is prop-erly important...

When you're writing about props and stage furniture that could be used for a production of *An Inspector Calls*, think about how the items you've chosen could help to send a particular message to the audience.

Sound

Sound designers are in charge of all the sound in a play — apart from the audience's (inevitable) applause.

Sound design should match the style of the production

1) Priestley <u>doesn't</u> include much information about sound in the <u>stage directions</u> for *An Inspector Calls*.

2) This gives sound designers the opportunity to be <u>creative</u>, but it's important that their <u>sound plot</u> is in keeping with the director's <u>vision</u> and the <u>style</u> of the production.

3) When creating a <u>sound plot</u>, a designer should think about how sound can:

> A sound plot is a plan of all the sounds and equipment used for a production. It also says when the sounds will be used.

- establish <u>setting</u> and <u>context</u>
- support <u>action on and off stage</u>
- create <u>tension</u> and <u>mood</u>
- aid <u>characterisation</u>

Sound can help establish the play's setting and context

1) The play begins as the Birlings finish an evening meal, so a <u>naturalistic</u> production might use a <u>pre-recorded soundscape</u> of <u>cutlery scraping</u> and <u>glasses clinking</u> to set the scene as the curtain rises.

> A soundscape is a collection of individual sounds that are layered up to give a strong sense of place.

2) If a fireplace has been included in the set design, the sound of the <u>fire crackling</u> could reinforce the feeling of <u>comfort</u> and the <u>relaxed atmosphere</u> of the dinner at the start of the play.

3) In Act Two, both Gerald and Eric leave the stage and the audience hears the front door "*slam*" each time. This sound effect would help to establish the setting as a room <u>within</u> the Birlings' house as well as implying that there's a world <u>beyond</u> the stage, which would add to the play's <u>realism</u>.

4) A <u>gramophone</u> could be placed on stage and used to play <u>music</u> from 1912, which would establish the play's <u>setting</u> in the early 20th century.

Non-naturalistic Sound

A <u>non-naturalistic</u> production could use sound to reflect the <u>context</u> in which the play was <u>written</u>. Recordings of <u>speeches by Hitler</u>, who led Germany into the <u>Second World War</u>, could be played in the background as Mr Birling tells his family "The Germans don't want war." This would reinforce the <u>dramatic irony</u> of this line by reminding the audience of the <u>historic events</u> yet to take place.

Sound can reinforce actions

1) Sound can be used to <u>signal</u> that something is happening on stage — these sounds are normally <u>diegetic</u> (heard by the characters) and can be made <u>live</u> or <u>pre-recorded</u>.

> As well as thinking about what sounds to include, a sound designer also needs to think about how to create them.

2) When the Inspector reappears at the end of Act One, a <u>creaking noise</u> could be played as "*The door slowly opens*". This ominous noise would <u>draw the audience's attention</u> to the Inspector's arrival as well as increasing the <u>tension</u>.

3) Sound can also be used to tell the audience about action happening <u>off stage</u>. The "*sharp ring of a front door bell*" in Act One <u>signals the arrival of a visitor</u> to the audience as well as the characters.

4) Sound can also highlight the <u>importance</u> of an action or event. At the end of Act Three "*The telephone rings sharply.*" A sound designer may choose to <u>amplify</u> the harsh ringing sound in order to highlight the <u>significance</u> of the moment.

Effect on the Audience

Diegetic sound effects that signal something happening off stage can make the play seem more <u>believable</u>. They encourage the audience to accept that there's a world <u>beyond</u> what they can <u>see</u> on stage.

Sound

Sound can create mood and tension

Non-diegetic sounds are sounds that don't exist in the world of the play and can't be heard by the characters.

1) <u>Non-diegetic sound</u> can be used to reflect the <u>mood</u> on stage. <u>Upbeat</u> background music could be played at the start of Act One to emphasise the <u>celebratory atmosphere</u> in the house.

2) The Inspector's arrival in Act One could be accompanied by <u>thunderclaps</u>. This would signal an abrupt <u>change in mood</u> and rapidly build the <u>tension</u> for the audience.

3) In the final moments of Act Two, as the Inspector reveals that Eva/Daisy was pregnant, <u>two sets of heartbeats</u> could be played in the background to suggest the heartbeats of Eva/Daisy and her baby. These heartbeats could build to a <u>climax</u> as the characters realise the identity of the baby's father, <u>stopping suddenly</u> as Eric enters the room. This would symbolise how the actions of the characters have <u>cut short</u> the lives of both Eva/Daisy and her unborn child.

© Vishal Sharma/Altrincham Garrick Playhouse

The Inspector's arrival may be accompanied by a change in the sound.

Sound can aid characterisation

1) The sounds played when characters are on stage can help the audience to form <u>opinions</u> about them.

2) <u>Underscoring</u> Mr Birling's monologues in Act One with <u>discordant</u> music could emphasise his <u>selfish</u> and <u>unpleasant</u> nature.

3) During the Inspector's last speech in Act Three, a soundscape of <u>explosions</u> and <u>bullets being fired</u> could be played. This would reinforce his <u>omniscience</u>, by implying that he <u>already knows</u> about the terrible loss that war will bring over the next few years.

Non-naturalistic Sound

An Inspector Calls can be viewed as a <u>morality play</u> (see p. 20), and the Birlings and Gerald could represent the <u>seven deadly sins</u>. A non-naturalistic production could emphasise this by using <u>pre-recorded whispers</u> to highlight the sin each character is guilty of as they confess. Playing whispers of '<u>envy</u>' as Sheila admits her role in Eva/Daisy's dismissal would highlight how <u>jealousy</u> drove her to act as she did.

Explain the effects of your design choices

When writing about <u>sound</u> in your exam, make sure you have a clear idea of <u>how</u> you would create each sound and the <u>effect</u> it would create for the audience.

> In Act One, Mr Birling's speech to Eric and Gerald is interrupted by the "sharp ring" of the doorbell. To create this effect, I would use a recorded sound of an old-fashioned doorbell, edited to be particularly high pitched, and play this at a loud volume. This would cut through Mr Birling's speech and distract the audience's attention, illustrating the power that the Inspector holds over the other characters before he has even entered the stage.

This uses <u>technical details</u> to precisely describe creating the <u>sound effect</u>.

This includes further details with its <u>intended effect</u>.

EXAM TIP

Gasps of horror reinforced the exam-hall setting...

When writing about sound design, you need to think about the balance of sound and dialogue — e.g. if a character is speaking quietly, any sound effects would also need to be quiet so the actor could be heard.

Lighting

Lighting lets the audience see what's happening on stage, but it can also help deliver important messages.

Lighting design should match the style of the production

1) Priestley provides <u>very few</u> details about lighting in the stage directions. This gives a designer a lot of <u>freedom</u> when choosing the lighting effects for a production of *An Inspector Calls*.

2) In a <u>naturalistic</u> production, the lighting should be as <u>realistic</u> as possible. This could be achieved by including <u>light sources</u>, such as lamps, <u>on stage</u>. When the lighting comes from a source <u>within the set</u>, it makes the setting feel more <u>convincing</u> for the audience.

3) In <u>non-naturalistic</u> productions, lighting doesn't need to be realistic, so designers can use lighting in more <u>abstract</u> ways for <u>dramatic effect</u>.

This production uses authentic wall lights to create naturalistic lighting.

Non-naturalistic Lighting

Several <u>Fresnel spotlights</u> moving across the stage and over the audience could be used to create the effect of <u>searchlights</u> as the Inspector approaches the Birlings' front door in Act One. This would highlight the <u>post-war context</u> in which the play was written, and could also imply that the Inspector has arrived to <u>seek out and reveal the family's secrets</u>.

Lighting can highlight action on stage...

Lighting is <u>essential</u> for making sure the audience can <u>see what's happening</u> on stage, but it can also be used to <u>direct the audience's attention</u> to key moments.

- The actor playing the Inspector could be <u>backlit</u> when he enters in Act One. Backlighting would cast the actor's face into <u>darkness</u>, which would make his entrance <u>mysterious</u> and <u>dramatic</u>.

- In Act Two, an <u>uplight</u> could <u>highlight</u> the moment that Sheila gives Gerald the ring back. The uplight would cast <u>shadows</u> across the actors' faces, which would reflect the <u>bitterness</u> felt by the characters.

- A <u>spotlight</u> could be shone over the phone when it rings in Act Three. The light could <u>flicker</u> in time with the ringing to highlight the <u>significance</u> of the phone call.

Effect on the Audience

<u>Darkness</u> can be just as <u>effective</u> as light for marking an important moment. When the Inspector exits the stage after delivering his warning in Act Three, a <u>blackout</u> could plunge the entire theatre into <u>darkness</u> for a few seconds. This would <u>shock</u> the audience and force them to <u>think</u> about what the Inspector has said. The <u>pause</u> in the action would also create <u>tension</u>, as the audience wonder what will happen next.

...and help to establish time and location

1) Mr Birling asks Edna to "<u>Give us some more light.</u>" before the Inspector makes his first entrance in Act One. This suggests that the events of the play are happening in the <u>early evening</u>. If the lighting design includes onstage lamps, the <u>intensity</u> of the lamps could be increased.

2) If a <u>fireplace</u> has been included in the set, a <u>Fresnel</u> shone through an <u>orange gel</u> could be used to cast an <u>orange glow</u> into the room. Creating the impression that a fire is <u>lit</u> would also suggest that the events are happening in the <u>early evening</u>.

3) A '<u>window</u>' could be <u>projected</u> onto the wall of the set using a <u>gobo</u>. The gobo could also include <u>tree silhouettes</u>, which would help to establish the location of the Birlings' house in a <u>leafy suburb</u> of Brumley.

Lighting

Lighting can help to support characterisation

1) A director could use lighting to emphasise the qualities of a particular character. For example, when Mr Birling tells Gerald and Eric how important it is for a man to "look after himself" in Act One, a parcan could cast cool blue washes of light on stage to reflect his uncaring, selfish nature.

2) Lighting can also be useful for revealing a character's status. When the Inspector asks "Are you sure you don't know?" in Act One, a downlight positioned at a shallow angle could be used to cast a large shadow behind him. This would emphasise the Inspector's power over the Birlings, as well as his mysterious, shadowy nature.

3) Relationships between characters can be reinforced by lighting, for example, when Sheila teases Gerald about his behaviour the previous summer in Act One, a rose-tinted wash could suggest the initial affection between the couple. This light could then flicker when Sheila delivers the line "Yes, that's what *you* say" to suggest that she is suspicious of Gerald, and hint at the cracks within their relationship.

4) Lighting can also be used to reveal a character's emotions. When Mr and Mrs Birling realise Eric's involvement with Eva/Daisy, they are both "*frightened*". Side lights could be shone onto the actors' faces to illuminate their features and make their frightened expressions more visible to the audience.

Non-naturalistic Lighting

From the line "To do my duty." until the end of Act Two, strobe lighting could be used to increase the intensity of the action. This style of lighting would also reinforce the fear and distress felt by the characters.

Using strobe lighting can make some people feel unwell. If strobe lighting is to be used, it's important that audience members are made aware.

Mood and atmosphere can be reinforced by lighting

1) Changes in lighting can indicate a shift in mood.

2) Priestley includes specific instructions about the lighting for before and after the Inspector arrives. The stage directions say that lighting should "*be pink and intimate*" at the start of Act One, and then become "*brighter and harder*" when the Inspector arrives.

Candlelight creates an intimate atmosphere at the start of Act One.

3) The pink lighting creates a cosy, warm atmosphere, reflecting the comfortable and relaxed mood as the characters celebrate Sheila and Gerald's engagement. The change to brighter, harder lighting when the Inspector arrives would create a tense atmosphere and emphasise the Inspector's intrusion upon the family's evening.

4) During Sheila's confession in Act One, the lights on the rest of the stage could fade, leaving a single profile spotlight on Sheila that intensifies as she delivers her monologue. This would create a reflective atmosphere, isolating Sheila and implying that she is speaking to herself as she recalls the memory. A sudden change to the original lighting arrangement as she delivers the line "I couldn't be sorry for her." would give the impression that she is snapping back to reality.

5) When Mrs Birling first enters the stage in Act Two, lighting could be used to reflect how she is "*quite out of key with the little scene that has just passed*". This could be done by shining a rose-tinted spotlight over Mrs Birling to represent her upbeat mood and to suggest that she is oblivious to the seriousness of Sheila and the Inspector's conversation.

Theatre of Cruelty

Theatre of Cruelty is a style of theatre which aims to make the audience feel extreme emotions through effects such as bright lights and loud noises. If a production of *An Inspector Calls* used this style of theatre, bright lights could be shone at the audience at the end of the play. This would be shocking, and may remind the audience that they might also be guilty of treating others badly, just like the Birlings.

Section Four — Staging and Design

Lighting

Lighting can be used symbolically

1) <u>Lighting</u> can be used <u>symbolically</u> to represent certain <u>themes</u> or <u>ideas</u>. As the Inspector recounts Eva/Daisy's death towards the end of Act Two, any lamps on stage could <u>flicker and then go out</u>, symbolising how Eva/Daisy's hopes were <u>extinguished</u> when Mrs Birling refused to help her.

2) In Act Three, from the line "There you are! Proof positive." until the end of the act, the lighting could gradually <u>fade</u>. The <u>increasing darkness</u> on stage could symbolise how some of the characters have <u>failed</u> to learn from their mistakes.

Lighting from above could symbolise the theme of judgement.

3) <u>Coloured</u> lighting can be used <u>symbolically</u> in non-naturalistic productions. For example, when Eric learns of his mother's involvement in Eva/Daisy's death at the start of Act Three, a light shone through a <u>red gel</u> would create a <u>red wash</u> across the stage. The colour red is associated with <u>anger and danger</u>, and this would emphasise Eric's <u>loss of control</u> as he angrily accuses his mother.

Practical Issues

When coloured lights <u>mix</u> with other colours on stage (for example, colours in the <u>scenery</u>, <u>stage furniture</u> or <u>costumes</u>) this may affect what the audience sees. For example, <u>red lights</u> can turn <u>green</u> objects <u>grey</u>, so a lighting designer needs to think <u>carefully</u> about the colours they use.

Include details about equipment when writing about lighting

When writing about lighting, it's important to include information about <u>technical equipment</u>.

> **This considers how the lighting will <u>suit</u> the <u>style</u> of the production.**
>
> At the start of the play, Priestley intended for the lighting on stage to be "*pink and intimate*", until the Inspector arrives when it should be "*brighter and harder.*" In order to complement a naturalistic style, I would create the initial pink lighting by including authentic 1910s-style wall lights which use pink lampshades within the set. The light generated would reflect off the lampshades, helping to make the intimate, rosy lighting that Priestley suggested. To create the change in lighting as the Inspector arrives, I would include a large ceiling light within the set above the stage. This would provide a naturalistic source of hard, bright light, which Edna could switch on as the Inspector enters the room.
>
> **This <u>explains</u> how the effect would be created.**
>
> **Give <u>precise details</u> about the lighting equipment you'd use.**

Still in the dark? Have a go at this revision task...

REVISION TASK

Imagine you're a lighting designer for a production of 'An Inspector Calls'. Write a paragraph about how you would use lighting to enhance the dramatic impact of the Inspector's warning just before he exits in Act Three. Remember to write about:

1) The atmosphere you are trying to create.
2) How you want the audience to feel during this scene.
3) What equipment you would use to create these effects.

Tick list:
- ✓ correct use of technical language
- ✓ points explained clearly and thoroughly

Section Four — Staging and Design

Costume

It's the costume designer's job to consider everything about a character's appearance.

Realistic costumes can reflect the play's context

1) Priestley intended for the characters to be dressed in "*evening dress of the period*" with the men in "*tails and white ties, not dinner jackets.*"

2) A costume designer might not stick to Priestley's instructions exactly, but a naturalistic production should use historically accurate fashion styles to make the costumes seem authentic.

3) The play is set in 1912, so the younger characters (Sheila, Eric and Gerald) might wear clothing that was fashionable at the time. The older characters (Arthur and Sybil) may wear clothing that was more typical of the late Victorian period to highlight the difference in the characters' ages.

> **Costume — Gerald**
>
> A director may dress Gerald in a costume that is more similar in style to Arthur's. This would emphasise how his views are similar to Arthur's.

	Victorian period	Early 20th century
Women	• Dresses were often made from heavy fabrics like velvet. They were usually floor length and gathered around the waist with a full skirt. • Necklines were square or rounded and fairly low, and large puff sleeves were common. • Small waists were fashionable, so bodices (the part of the body of the dress above the waist) were tightly fitted. • Hair was pinned up, often with curls fluffed over the forehead. Chokers (tight necklaces) and brooches were very popular. Wealthy women might also wear pearl necklaces.	• Lighter fabrics such as tulle and chiffon became popular. Dresses continued to be floor length, but skirts became less full. • Necklines were low, and bodices would often have detailing on them in a V-shape towards the waist. Sleeves were often elbow length. • Loose dresses with lots of frills and lace known as tea dresses were fashionable. • Hair continued to be piled on top of the head. Women often wore elbow-length white gloves.
Men	• Formal evening wear included long, black tail coats worn with a white shirt and black trousers. Turned-up collars with thick knotted ties or cravats (similar to scarves) were popular. • Men's hair was usually short and well trimmed. Bushy sideburns and a short beard were popular.	• Formal evening wear remained similar to the Victorian period. Stiff, turned down collars (known as 'wing tips') were common, and ties were thinner. • Men's hair continued to be short and well trimmed. It became more popular for younger men to be clean-shaven, or to have a moustache.

Costume can show differences in status

1) The Birlings belong to the middle class, so their costumes should reflect their wealth and position in society by using fairly luxurious fabrics and expensive-looking accessories.

2) Gerald is a member of the upper class, so a costume designer may wish to hint that he is socially superior to the Birlings by making his costume grander than theirs — he could carry an elaborate pocket watch or wear an elegant pair of cufflinks.

©Vishal Sharma/Altrincham Garrick Playhouse

3) As a servant, Edna would probably wear a simple, dark-coloured dress and a white apron. This would contrast with the Birlings' impressive costumes and show that she is a member of the working class.

4) The stage directions suggest that the Inspector should be dressed in "*a plain darkish suit of the period*". The Inspector is mysterious and doesn't seem to belong to a social class, so this costume would reflect this by not revealing much about him.

Costume

Costumes often reveal information about a character...

1) Costume can reflect a character's <u>age</u> and <u>personality</u>. For example, Mrs Birling could be dressed <u>modestly</u> — her dress may have a <u>higher neckline</u> to reflect her <u>maturity</u>. Dressing Mrs Birling in <u>darker colours</u> could also reflect her <u>sterner, less forgiving attitude</u>.

2) In contrast, a designer might dress Sheila in a <u>pale pink, frilly dress</u>. This would make her appear <u>youthful</u> and <u>feminine</u>, as well as suggesting that she takes <u>pride in her appearance</u>. A designer may also give Sheila <u>expensive-looking jewellery</u> to hint at her <u>materialistic</u> nature.

Sheila's floaty dress emphasises her femininity.

©Vishal Sharma/Altrincham Garrick Playhouse

3) Costume designers should also consider how <u>smaller details</u> can convey information about the characters to the audience. Giving the actors playing Mr and Mrs Birling <u>wigs with streaks of grey</u> would help to convey their <u>age</u> to the audience. Including <u>extra padding</u> in their costumes to make them look larger might help to reflect their <u>comfortable and extravagant lifestyle</u>.

Practical Issues

Designers also need to think about the <u>practicalities</u> of their costumes, including whether they allow <u>easy movement</u> on stage, and how <u>comfortable</u> they are for the actors.

... and might show how they change

1) At the start of the play, Sheila's hair could be <u>immaculately styled</u> in the fashion of the period — this hairstyle could <u>loosen</u> and <u>fall down</u> as the play progresses to show that she is finding the Inspector's questions <u>stressful</u>, as well as suggesting she is becoming <u>less concerned</u> about her <u>outward appearance</u>.

2) Eric's shirt could be <u>pristine and tidy</u> at the start of the play, but by the end of Act Three, it could become <u>crumpled</u> and <u>untucked</u>. This could show how he can no longer <u>keep up appearances</u> and hide his <u>true character</u> from his family.

3) Mr Birling could <u>remove</u> his jacket when the Inspector questions him to hint at his <u>worry</u>. After the phone call to the hospital in Act Three, Mr Birling could put his jacket <u>back on</u> to show how he thinks everything is <u>back to normal</u>.

At the end of this production, Mr and Mrs Birling's costumes are in disarray.

© Donald Cooper/ photostage

Costume can have a symbolic meaning

1) Designers can use costume to <u>symbolise</u> something about a character for the audience.

2) Eric could wear a <u>black</u> bow tie which would <u>contrast</u> with the <u>white</u> bow ties worn by Gerald and Mr Birling. This would hint at Eric's <u>rebellious</u> nature, and could symbolise how he is a <u>black sheep</u> (someone who brings disrepute to their family).

3) The actor playing the Inspector could wear <u>tap plates</u> on his shoes to amplify the noise he makes when walking around the stage. This could be used to symbolise his <u>authority</u> and reinforce the way he <u>commands the attention</u> of the other characters.

4) Mr Birling's jacket could be <u>stained with food</u> and his shoes could be <u>scuffed</u>. This would symbolise how he is not the <u>upstanding member of society</u> that he thinks he is.

Costume — Eva/Daisy

Some productions may choose to show <u>Eva/Daisy</u> on stage. A costume designer could use <u>colour symbolism</u> in her costume. For example, a <u>white dress</u> could highlight Eva/Daisy's <u>innocence</u>, whereas a <u>drab, grey</u> dress could symbolise how she has been <u>disregarded</u> and <u>ignored</u> by society.

Costume

Make-up can be used to add to a character's appearance

1) Make-up is an important part of a character's costume. It can highlight aspects of their physical appearance and personality or show changes in their emotions and attitudes.

2) Make-up could be used to show Mr and Mrs Birling's age, especially if they are being played by younger actors, for example by using latex wrinkles.

3) Dark eye shadow could be smudged under Eric's eyes to suggest his heavy drinking is making him unwell.

4) Sheila might at first have soft, pastel-coloured make-up to show her youth and femininity. Make-up could then be used to reflect her distress when she re-enters the stage after seeing Eva/Daisy's photograph in Act One. A make-up artist could use streaks of mascara around her eyes to create the impression that she has been crying.

Non-naturalistic costumes can represent themes or ideas

1) Unlike naturalistic productions, non-naturalistic productions don't need to be historically accurate, so a designer can have more freedom over the choice of costumes.

2) A designer can use costumes to emphasise aspects of a character or highlight the play's themes.

> • The Inspector could wear a bloodied military uniform to suggest he has witnessed the First and Second World Wars. This would reinforce the supernatural elements of the Inspector's character by suggesting that he has travelled back in time to warn the Birlings about their actions. This would also highlight the foolishness of Mr Birling's belief that war will not happen.
>
> • Dressing the characters in plain clothes that don't suggest a particular time period could highlight how the play's themes and message could be relevant to any time period.

In the exam, think about what costume says about a character

Here's an example of how you could write about Sheila's costume:

> This explains how your choices reflect aspects of Sheila's character.
>
> This shows the effect on the audience.

I would dress Sheila in a tea dress made of loose and lightweight fabrics. This would complement a naturalistic performance whilst simultaneously highlighting Sheila's wealth through her ability to follow current fashion trends. The lightweight fabrics would help to demonstrate her carefree attitude, whilst a pale colour such as light pink would help to emphasise her naivety and youth to the audience. Her hair could be elaborately styled on top of her head, emphasising her middle-class status as well as hinting at her vain nature by suggesting that she spends a lot of free time on her appearance, rather than having to work.

> This shows you've considered the play's context.
>
> It's good to show that you've considered smaller details in your costume design.

EXAM TIP

Writing about costume is sew easy...

When you're writing about costume design, remember to think about how smaller details can convey meaning to the audience. You also need to make sure that your ideas match the production's style.

Section Four — Staging and Design

Practice Questions

Imagine a play with no sound, lighting, costumes or scenery. Pretty boring, eh? Before you move on to Section Five, work your way through these questions to check you know your gobos from your rostra.

Quick Questions

1) Name two practicalities that a director should consider when choosing a stage type for a production of *An Inspector Calls*.

2) Give two examples of how a non-naturalistic production could use entrances and exits to enhance a performance of *An Inspector Calls*.

3) Give one reason why a set designer might use levels in *An Inspector Calls*.

4) Give one example of how a prop is used to drive the action in the play.

5) What is the difference between diegetic and non-diegetic sound?

6) How might sound be used to represent an aspect of a character? Give one example.

7) What could a designer use to light the stage in a naturalistic production of the play?

8) What is the effect of the change in stage lighting when the Inspector enters in Act One?

9) Give one example of how a designer might use a character's costume to create symbolism.

In-depth Questions

1) Choose a stage type and explain why you think it would be appropriate for staging a production of *An Inspector Calls*. Use examples from the play to back up your answer.

2) How might a set designer use colour symbolism in a non-naturalistic production of *An Inspector Calls*? Explain the reasons behind your ideas.

3) How might a sound designer contribute to the sense of triumph and excitement after the family find out the Inspector wasn't a real police inspector in Act Three? Explain your answer.

4) How might a lighting designer use colour symbolism in a non-naturalistic production? Explain why your ideas are appropriate.

5) How might a costume designer dress Gerald to show that he is an upper-class character?

Practice Questions

What's that? You simply can't get enough of these hugely enjoyable questions and you'd like some longer exam-style ones to really stretch yourself on the subject of staging and design? Well, you're in luck...

Exam-style Questions

> Find the part of Act One where the Birlings and Gerald are talking after dinner. Read from Mr Birling "***raising his glass***" to where Gerald says "**I believe you're right, sir.**", then answer Question 1 below.

1) Imagine you're directing a production of *An Inspector Calls*. Explain how you would use props and stage furniture to portray this extract effectively on stage for the audience. In your answer, you should refer to the play's context.

> Find the part of Act One where Mr Birling's speech is interrupted by the arrival of the Inspector. Read from where Mr Birling says "**But this is the point.**" to where the Inspector says "**Quite so.**", then answer Question 2 below.

2) Imagine you are a lighting designer working on a production of *An Inspector Calls*. Describe how you would use lighting design to add to the overall impact of this extract on the audience.

> Find the part of Act Two where the Inspector says "**Where had he got it from then?**" to the end of the act, then answer Question 3 below.

3) Imagine you're directing a production of *An Inspector Calls*. Explain how you would use staging to portray this extract effectively for the audience. In your answer, you should refer to the play's context.

> Find the part of Act Three where the Birlings are thinking about calling the hospital. Read from where Mr Birling says "**It will look a bit queer, won't it**" to the end of the act, then answer Question 4 below.

4) Imagine you are a sound designer working on a production of *An Inspector Calls*. Describe how you would use sound design to contribute to the overall impact of this extract on the audience.

Section Five — Close Analysis

Act One

This section analyses key moments in the play and suggests how performance skills and design features can communicate meaning to the audience — the same sort of thing you'll need to do in the exam.

The Inspector interrupts the celebratory mood in Act One

1) Act One is important for <u>setting the tone</u> of the whole play — the <u>arrival</u> of the Inspector <u>interrupts</u> a <u>warm</u>, <u>celebratory atmosphere</u> and creates a <u>tense</u>, <u>unsettled mood</u> which continues throughout the <u>rest of the play</u>.

2) At the start of the act, as the Birlings are celebrating Sheila and Gerald's engagement, the atmosphere is <u>upbeat</u> and <u>intimate</u>.

3) This mood is <u>disrupted</u> by the Inspector's arrival. The "*sharp ring*" of the doorbell which signals his arrival <u>interrupts</u> Mr Birling mid-speech, suggesting that the Inspector will <u>disturb</u> the family's <u>pleasant evening</u>.

4) The <u>tension</u> of the act <u>develops</u> as the Inspector starts to question Mr Birling about the death of Eva/Daisy. Birling becomes increasingly <u>frustrated</u> and <u>annoyed</u>, which creates an <u>uncomfortable atmosphere</u>.

5) <u>Sheila</u> is then questioned by the Inspector and becomes <u>distressed</u> as her part in Eva/Daisy's <u>death</u> is revealed. Sheila's <u>character</u> begins to <u>develop</u> as she takes responsibility for her actions.

The Birlings are celebrating at the start of Act One.

6) Act One closes with a <u>duologue</u> between Sheila and Gerald — Sheila's <u>suspicions</u> about Gerald <u>knowing</u> Eva/Daisy are <u>confirmed</u>, and she warns that <u>worse</u> is yet to come in the Inspector's <u>interrogations</u>. This creates an <u>ominous mood</u> and a <u>sense of foreboding</u> as the play moves into Act Two.

Mr Birling gives a speech about business and war

1) Arthur Birling <u>dominates</u> the early part of Act One — he gives <u>long monologues</u> about his <u>opinions</u>.

2) An actor could use a <u>confident tone</u> and speak at a <u>higher volume</u> to show Mr Birling's <u>pomposity</u> and how he likes to <u>hear himself talk</u>.

3) <u>Stressing</u> the words "<u>I</u>" and "<u>my</u>" in Mr Birling's speech would emphasise his sense of <u>self-importance</u> to the audience.

4) An actor could deliver Birling's monologues using a <u>regular pace</u>. This would suggest that he's a <u>confident</u> character and he's comfortable being the <u>centre of attention</u>.

Sound Design — Music

- <u>Cheerful music</u> from the <u>time period</u> (1912) could be used to reflect the <u>happy</u> atmosphere at the start of Act One. It could be <u>non-diegetic</u> (see p. 57), or it could appear to come from an <u>onstage source</u>, e.g. a <u>gramophone</u>.

- <u>Non-diegetic music</u> featuring <u>bugles</u>, <u>marching drums</u> and <u>fanfares</u> could be used to <u>underscore</u> Mr Birling's monologues. Using music with <u>military connotations</u> could highlight the <u>dramatic irony</u> of his opinion that <u>war won't happen</u>.

5) Mr Birling asks rhetorical <u>questions</u> during his speeches (e.g. "<u>And why?</u>"), which don't require an answer from the other characters. This suggests that he's <u>self-absorbed</u> — he only wants to hear his <u>own voice</u>, not other people's <u>views</u>. An actor playing Mr Birling could emphasise this by <u>pausing</u> very briefly after each question, as if to allow the other characters to answer, before giving the answer <u>himself</u>.

Effect on the Audience

In Act One, the audience is likely to find Arthur Birling <u>arrogant</u> and <u>foolish</u>. The more <u>unsympathetic</u> he is, the more they'll be encouraged to <u>side</u> with the <u>Inspector</u> when he arrives, rather than Birling.

Act One

The Inspector questions Mr Birling and Sheila

1) The Inspector arrives and starts to <u>question</u> the family — he speaks first to Mr Birling and then to Sheila. An actor playing the Inspector could use their <u>tone of voice</u> to highlight the Inspector's <u>control</u> over the situation.

2) The <u>stage directions</u> describe him speaking "*carefully*" and "*weightily*". An actor could use an <u>even</u>, <u>curt tone</u> and a <u>steady pace</u> to make his words seem <u>important</u> and emphasise that he is <u>calm</u> and <u>authoritative</u>.

3) The Inspector uses certain lines to <u>mock</u> Mr Birling's selfish views (e.g. "<u>Very awkward.</u>"). An actor could use a <u>sarcastic tone</u> on these lines to make his feelings clear.

© Vishal Sharma/Altrincham Garrick Playhouse

Set Design — Props

- A designer could make the "*postcard size*" photograph of Eva/Daisy <u>yellowed</u>, <u>worn</u> and <u>creased</u>. Since the photograph is the only <u>physical</u> object on stage linked to Eva/Daisy, making it appear <u>worn</u> and <u>fragile</u> could reflect how she was <u>mistreated</u> and <u>worn down</u> by the Birlings and Gerald.

- The Inspector's <u>notebook</u> could be used to reflect how <u>focused</u> he is. Using a smart but well-used notebook with lots of writing in would suggest how <u>seriously</u> he takes his task.

Sheila and Gerald speak privately

1) When the Inspector and Eric <u>leave</u> the room, Sheila and Gerald are <u>alone</u>, and they <u>speak privately</u> about Gerald's <u>connection</u> to Eva/Daisy. A <u>designer</u> could use <u>lighting</u> to make their duologue more <u>dramatic</u>.

2) When the Inspector exits, the "*brighter and harder*" lighting used to mark his entrance earlier in the act could return to the "*pink and intimate*" lighting used at the start of the play. This would suggest that Sheila and Gerald feel <u>less threatened</u> and more able to <u>speak freely</u> with the Inspector out of the room. This <u>warm, pink wash</u> could be created using a <u>floodlight</u> and <u>pink gels</u>.

3) The <u>pink wash</u> could slowly become <u>redder</u> to reflect the <u>growing tension</u> between the two characters.

4) A <u>profile spotlight</u> could be used to <u>illuminate</u> the Inspector as "*The door slowly opens*", and the rest of the lighting could be <u>dimmed</u>. This would take the audience's focus <u>away</u> from Sheila and Gerald, and direct their attention <u>toward</u> the Inspector's <u>sudden entrance</u>.

Physical Skills — Proxemics

- When the <u>duologue</u> starts, Gerald could stand <u>further away</u> from Sheila by the sideboard, while she remains <u>frozen on the spot</u>. This could represent her <u>shock</u> at realising he <u>knew Daisy Renton</u>.

- When Gerald says "<u>Now listen, darling —</u>" while "*approaching*" Sheila, an actor playing Sheila could <u>move away</u> to show how she <u>refuses</u> to be <u>patronised</u> or <u>lied to</u>.

- When Sheila <u>interrogates</u> Gerald about Eva/Daisy, an actor could show her <u>anger</u> by <u>moving back closer</u> to him and <u>gripping his arm firmly</u> as if she's trying to <u>force</u> him to <u>confess</u>.

- When the Inspector returns to the stage, he could stand <u>uncomfortably close</u> to Gerald and Sheila. This could reflect how he has <u>intruded</u> upon their lives.

EXAM TIP

This is one of my three favourite acts in the entire play...

All the choices made for a production have a big impact on how an audience interprets the play. It's important to think carefully about how each decision adds to the overall effect of the performance.

Act Two

No time passes between each act in the play, so Act Two picks up right where Act One left off. The Inspector is ready to ask some more questions, and this time it's Gerald and Sybil who have to answer...

Act Two builds conflict between the characters

1) In Act Two, the <u>relationships</u> between the characters are put <u>under pressure</u> by the Inspector's <u>questions</u>.

2) The <u>different</u> ways that the characters <u>react</u> to the revelations show how the <u>divide</u> between the characters is <u>widening</u>.

3) Gerald eventually <u>accepts</u> that he needs to be <u>honest</u> with the Inspector, and he reveals the <u>truth</u> about his affair with Eva/Daisy.

4) Mrs Birling, however, responds to the Inspector's questions <u>rudely</u> and is <u>reluctant</u> to talk about her part in Eva/Daisy's death.

© Pete Jones / ArenaPAL

5) Sheila, meanwhile, becomes more <u>cynical</u>, <u>sarcastic</u> and <u>emotional</u> as the act progresses, which shows how <u>strongly</u> she's been <u>affected</u> by the Inspector. She's <u>blunt</u> and <u>sarcastic</u> with Gerald — their relationship has <u>deteriorated</u> significantly since the start of Act One.

6) The characters have <u>different reactions</u> to the Inspector's message of <u>social responsibility</u>. This <u>increases the tension</u> and hints at the <u>conflict</u> to come between the characters at the end of Act Three.

7) When the Inspector reveals that <u>Eva/Daisy</u> was <u>pregnant</u> with Eric Birling's child at the end of the act, Mrs Birling's <u>shock</u> and <u>distress</u> creates an <u>emotional climax</u> for the audience.

Gerald admits his affair with Eva/Daisy

1) At first, Gerald tries to <u>resist</u> the Inspector's questions, but he quickly realises that he needs to <u>admit</u> to his affair with Eva, who he knew as <u>Daisy Renton</u>. A sound designer could use a variety of <u>techniques</u> to make his confession more <u>dramatic</u>.

2) In a <u>non-naturalistic</u> production, <u>non-diegetic</u> sounds could be used while Gerald is speaking to make his account more <u>vivid</u>. For example, a pre-recorded track of <u>glasses</u> and <u>cutlery clinking</u> could be used when Gerald describes how he and Daisy went to the <u>County Hotel</u>.

3) <u>Incidental music</u> could <u>underscore</u> Gerald's monologue where he describes how he found Eva/Daisy somewhere to live. The music could be <u>light and romantic</u> which would emphasise Gerald's <u>tender</u> feelings towards Eva/Daisy, as well as suggesting that this was a <u>happy time</u> in her life.

4) In a <u>naturalistic</u> production, <u>diegetic</u> sounds could be used. As Gerald confesses, the sound of <u>rain</u> lashing against a window could be played to suggest <u>stormy weather</u> outside which could symbolise Gerald's <u>distress</u> and <u>sadness</u>. The sounds of <u>wind</u> or <u>thunder</u> could also be used to <u>mark</u> particularly <u>important</u> or <u>emotional moments</u> in his confession. Using sound in this way would also make his <u>exit</u> more <u>dramatic</u>, as the audience would understand that he is <u>too distressed</u> to care about going outside in the bad weather.

Vocal Skills — Gerald

- Gerald <u>speaks openly</u> about his actions — an actor could speak <u>clearly</u> with a <u>regular pace</u> to show how he is <u>resigned to his fate</u>.

- Speaking his lines <u>quietly</u> while he admits to his part in Eva/Daisy's suicide could show Gerald's <u>respect</u> for her and his <u>regret</u> at her death.

- Though he usually <u>seems composed</u>, an actor might make Gerald's voice <u>crack with emotion</u> when he says "<u>My God!</u>" to show his <u>distress</u> when it <u>hits him</u> for the first time that Eva/Daisy has really <u>died</u>.

Act Two

Mrs Birling is questioned by the Inspector

1) Mrs Birling enters <u>confidently</u> while Gerald is being questioned — she's been <u>offstage</u> during the <u>revelations</u> of Act One, and doesn't realise the <u>seriousness</u> of the situation. She's soon <u>appalled</u> by the Inspector's <u>lack of respect</u>, and an actor playing Sybil could use <u>physical skills</u> to show this.

2) An actor could enter with a <u>wide smile</u> which <u>fades</u> when Mrs Birling realises the Inspector can't be <u>intimidated</u>. <u>Proxemics</u> could show Sybil's <u>dislike</u> of the Inspector, e.g. by <u>increasing the space</u> between them.

3) Mrs Birling tries to stay <u>composed</u>, but she soon begins to <u>falter</u>. When Sheila and Arthur <u>criticise</u> her, an actor playing her could <u>look quickly</u> at them and <u>back</u> to the Inspector to show her <u>growing panic</u>, but continue to <u>stand still</u> — this would show that she's trying to <u>look calm</u>, but she's actually <u>distressed</u>.

4) <u>Levels</u> could be used to show how the Inspector is more <u>powerful</u> than Mrs Birling and how he is <u>judging</u> her. She could <u>sit down</u> when she becomes "<u>cowed</u>" by the Inspector's <u>anger</u>. The Inspector could <u>stay standing</u>, forcing her to <u>look up at him</u>.

Effect on the Audience

Mrs Birling's <u>ignorance</u> of the Inspector's <u>determined</u> nature creates <u>dramatic irony</u> for the audience — they have seen his questioning of Mr Birling and Sheila and <u>know</u> he won't let Mrs Birling <u>intimidate</u> him.

Staging — Non-naturalistic Scenery

- A <u>backdrop</u> showing a <u>silhouette</u> of Eva/Daisy with a <u>baby</u> might make Sybil's cruel <u>treatment</u> of Eva/Daisy more <u>vivid</u> to the audience.
- A set of <u>wheeled flats</u> could be <u>turned round</u> during Sybil's questioning to <u>transform</u> the <u>dining room</u> into a <u>white</u>, <u>tiled infirmary</u> which would <u>remind</u> the <u>audience</u> of Eva/Daisy's <u>death</u>.

Mrs Birling accidentally condemns Eric

1) Mrs Birling is <u>tricked</u> by the Inspector into <u>condemning</u> Eric — she says that the <u>young man</u> who got Eva/Daisy pregnant and gave her stolen money should be <u>held accountable</u>. When she realises that it's Eric, she becomes <u>distressed</u> and <u>frightened</u>. <u>Staging</u> could be used to <u>intensify</u> this moment.

2) Performing the play on a <u>thrust stage</u> could allow Sybil to <u>separate</u> herself from the rest of the characters while she <u>confidently insists</u> that the young man is <u>responsible</u>. Moving to the <u>front</u> of the <u>apron</u> and leaving the other characters <u>upstage</u> would show how she's <u>isolated</u> and <u>trapped</u> when she <u>realises</u> that Eric is to blame.

3) When Eric enters at the <u>end</u> of the act, he could access the stage via <u>walkways</u> through the audience. As Eric walks past, audience members would turn to <u>look at him</u> which would reinforce the idea that he is being <u>judged</u>.

© Jane Hobson/REX/Shutterstock

Set Design — Lighting

- A lighting designer could use a <u>gobo</u> to cast stripes of <u>shadow</u> over Sybil to <u>represent prison bars</u>. This would hint at her <u>guilt</u> and suggest she is becoming <u>trapped</u> by the Inspector.
- As Act Two reaches its <u>climax</u>, a lighting designer could slowly <u>fade out the downlight</u> from <u>above</u> the stage while <u>intensifying the uplight</u> from the <u>floor lanterns</u>. This would gradually light the actors from <u>below</u>, casting <u>shadows</u> on their <u>faces</u> and creating a <u>menacing atmosphere</u>.

EXAM TIP

The Inspector would probably be great at close analysis...

He's always asking about the 'how' and 'why' of things. When you're thinking about a performance skill or design feature, think about why it might be used, what effect it has and how it creates that effect.

Act Three

Act Three consists of a long monologue from Edna where she explains how to scour a greasy pan. No, not really — the Inspector questions Eric, gives a speech, then exits, leaving the stage set for the play's final twist.

Act Three builds to the play's climax and final twist

1) In Act Three, the audience learns that Eric met Eva/Daisy — it is implied that he then <u>raped</u> her and got her <u>pregnant</u>. He also <u>stole money</u> from his father's company. These revelations are some of the most <u>emotional</u> of the play.

2) The tension <u>continues to build</u> as the family argue and the Inspector gives his <u>final warning</u> that if the Birlings and society don't <u>learn</u> to <u>look after</u> each other, then they will be <u>taught</u> the lesson in "<u>fire and blood and anguish</u>".

Effect on the Audience

The Inspector's final speech would have reminded <u>1940s audiences</u> about the <u>horrors</u> of World War Two (p. 8-9).

Effect on the Audience

By the <u>end</u> of the play, the audience may feel <u>contempt</u> and <u>frustration</u> towards Mr and Mrs Birling and Gerald because they're <u>unwilling to change</u>. The final phone call suggests that the characters are going to face <u>real-life consequences</u> for their actions, which could be <u>satisfying</u> for the audience.

3) After the Inspector <u>leaves</u>, the characters find out he wasn't a <u>real</u> inspector and that <u>no-one died</u> in the infirmary. At this point, it seems as though the play will end with an <u>anticlimax</u> — Mr and Mrs Birling and Gerald are <u>relieved</u> and <u>triumphant</u>, and think all their problems are <u>over</u>.

4) However, when the <u>phone rings</u> and it's revealed that a <u>real inspector</u> is on his way to ask about a girl who has <u>died</u> in the infirmary, the <u>tension returns</u> immediately. The play ends on an <u>shocking</u> and <u>unnerving</u> note.

Eric confesses to his part in Eva/Daisy's fate

1) Eric is <u>agitated</u> when he returns to the house and begins to be <u>questioned</u>. After <u>confessing</u> what he did to Eva/Daisy, he learns that Mrs Birling <u>refused</u> to help her, and he becomes incredibly <u>distressed</u> and <u>angry</u> with his mother. This change could be reflected in Eric's <u>costume</u> and <u>make-up</u>.

Costume Design

- During his questioning, an actor playing Eric could <u>dishevel</u> his appearance by <u>loosening his collar</u> and <u>removing his tie</u> to make his <u>stress</u> clear to the audience.

- When Eric answers the Inspector's questions "<u>miserably</u>", he could <u>run his hands</u> through his <u>hair</u> to reflect his <u>distress</u> and <u>intense emotion</u>.

- A designer might use <u>make-up</u> to make Eric appear <u>pale</u> and give him <u>shadows</u> under his eyes to suggest his <u>agitation</u> and show that he's "<u>extremely pale and distressed</u>".

© Simon Gough Photography

2) When Eric becomes <u>angry</u> with Mrs Birling, the scene becomes very <u>tense</u> and <u>emotional</u>. Actors could use <u>physical skills</u> to <u>emphasise</u> their dialogue:

Physical Skills — Gestures

- An actor playing Eric could <u>jab</u> at Mrs Birling <u>violently</u> with a <u>finger</u> while shouting at her to show his <u>uncontrollable emotion</u>, and how he holds his mother <u>accountable</u> for Eva/Daisy's death.

- When Mr Birling is described as "<u>furious, intervening</u>", an actor playing him could move toward Eric with <u>arms outstretched</u> and <u>hands open</u> as if to seize Eric <u>violently</u> by the <u>shoulders</u>.

- The Inspector is described as "<u>taking charge, masterfully</u>", saying "<u>Stop!</u>". An actor could slowly <u>lift an arm</u>, with his <u>palm facing down</u>, to show his <u>authority</u> and how <u>effortlessly</u> he can restore <u>order</u>.

Act Three

The Inspector delivers his final warning

1) Before the Inspector <u>leaves</u>, he gives the Birlings a powerful <u>final speech</u> about <u>social responsibility</u> and the <u>dangers</u> of not <u>changing</u> their behaviour.

2) An actor playing the Inspector could deliver his lines using a <u>regular pace</u> and a <u>normal volume</u>. <u>Juxtaposing</u> the Inspector's <u>calmness</u> with Eric's <u>frantic</u> and <u>angry behaviour</u> earlier in the act could make his message seem <u>sensible</u> and <u>rational</u>.

Set Design — Special Effects

- <u>A film reel of footage</u> showing working-class people from the <u>early 20th-century</u> could play during the Inspector's last speech. This would emphasise his <u>message</u> about <u>everyone deserving kindness</u> and remind the audience of how the play <u>relates to real life</u>.

- A designer could <u>project</u> an <u>image</u> of the Inspector <u>speaking</u> onto a <u>cyclorama</u> after he exits — his picture on the large curved screen would suggest that his <u>words</u> will continue to <u>haunt</u> the Birlings long after he <u>leaves</u>.

3) Alternatively, the Inspector could deliver his final speech in the style of a <u>preacher</u>, using a <u>louder volume</u>, a <u>quick pace</u> and a <u>changeable</u>, <u>musical intonation</u>, to make his words seem more <u>important</u>.

4) An actor playing the Inspector could place <u>stress</u> on the words "<u>our</u>" and "<u>we</u>" and <u>gesture</u> towards the <u>audience</u>. This would suggest that the Inspector is not only trying to <u>persuade</u> the <u>characters</u> on stage, but that he is also <u>addressing</u> the <u>audience</u>. This might encourage the audience to think about the <u>consequences</u> of their <u>own behaviour</u>.

The family think they're in the clear — until the phone rings...

1) When Gerald <u>returns</u> and <u>explains</u> to the Birlings his theory that the Inspector was a <u>hoax</u>, Mr and Mrs Birling become <u>excited</u>, and the <u>mood</u> on stage changes from <u>tension</u> to <u>relief</u>.

2) However, the play's <u>final twist</u> makes the mood <u>tense</u> again very <u>suddenly</u>. Actors could use <u>physical skills</u> and <u>interactions</u> between characters to communicate this <u>rapid change</u> in mood <u>effectively</u>.

© Paul Lovelace/REX/Shutterstock

- When Mr Birling calls the Chief Constable, an actor playing Birling could <u>nod enthusiastically</u> and visibly <u>relax his posture</u> by <u>dropping his shoulders</u>.

- When Birling <u>announces</u> that "There's no Inspector Goole on the police.", Gerald and Mrs Birling could let their own <u>shoulders and arms hang</u> more <u>loosely</u>, and <u>visibly exhale</u> to help to communicate their <u>relief</u> to the audience.

- Sheila and Eric are <u>disgusted</u> and <u>frightened</u> by the <u>triumphant attitude</u> taken by their parents and Gerald. <u>Closed body language</u> could be used to emphasise the <u>conflict</u> between the characters. Eric and Sheila could stand with their <u>arms folded</u>, or <u>shoulders hunched</u>, on the <u>other side of the stage</u> from their parents and Gerald. They could also <u>shake their heads</u> in <u>disbelief</u>.

- When the <u>phone rings</u>, the characters could all <u>freeze suddenly</u> and <u>look towards</u> it. This would communicate their <u>surprise</u>, and their <u>similar reactions</u> would also show that, despite their <u>differences</u>, they are all <u>equally shocked</u> and <u>worried</u> by the phone call.

EXAM TIP

And the moral of the story is — never answer the door...

A lot happens in Act Three, but try not to get thrown off by it — keep your exam answer focused on the question you've been asked. Have a clear aim in mind and make sure all your decisions support it.

Practice Questions

You're probably ready for a breather after all that close analysis, but don't reach for the TV remote just yet — you'll enjoy that episode of 'I'm An Inspector... Get Me Out of Here!' much more if you do these questions first.

Quick Questions

1) What kind of atmosphere might a director try to create before the Inspector's arrival in Act One?

2) What would be the effect of an actor playing Mr Birling placing stress on the words "I" and "my" in his speeches at the beginning of Act One?

3) Why might a prop designer choose to make the photograph of Eva/Daisy worn with age?

4) Why might a sound designer choose to play rain and storm sounds during Gerald's confession in Act Two?

5) Give two ways an actor playing Sybil could use physical skills to show that she is agitated by the Inspector in Act Two.

6) Give one way a lighting designer could create a menacing atmosphere at the end of Act Two.

7) Suggest a gesture an actor could use to show Eric's distress at the start of Act Three.

8) Give an example of how the Inspector could use vocal skills to suggest that he is talking to the audience as well as the characters in his final speech.

9) Describe a physical skill an actor playing Gerald could use to show his relief when Mr Birling phones the Chief Constable towards the end of Act Three.

In-depth Questions

1) Explain how sound could be used to create a celebratory atmosphere at the start of Act One.

2) Describe a costume design for Eric in Act One, then explain how this costume could change in Act Three. Discuss the effect of these changes on the audience.

3) Explain how an actor playing Sheila might use vocal skills effectively during her duologue with Gerald at the end of Act One.

4) Explain two ways in which you would use lighting to create a tense atmosphere at the end of Act Two.

5) How could special effects be used to enhance the Inspector's final speech in Act Three?

Practice Questions

It's time for the last set of exam-style questions in the book. You know the score by now — spend a good amount of time on each question, and try to write detailed analysis similar to the sort of thing you've read in this section. Solid preparation now will avoid ~~fire and blood and~~ anguish in the actual exam...

Exam-style Questions

> Find the part of Act One where the Birlings are celebrating. Read from where Mr Birling says "**Well, well — this is very nice.**" to where Eric says "**Good old Sheila!**", then answer Questions 1 and 2 below.

1) Imagine you're an actor playing Mrs Birling. She's described as being a cold person. Explain how you would use performance skills to portray her in this extract. Provide a reason for each of your examples.

2) Imagine you're a lighting designer working on a production of *An Inspector Calls*. Describe how you would use lighting design to add to the overall impact of this extract on the audience.

> Find the part of Act Two where Gerald is being questioned. Read from where he says "**I happened to look in, one night**" to where Sheila says "**Don't mind Mother.**", then answer Questions 3 and 4 below.

3) Imagine you're directing a production of *An Inspector Calls*. Explain how a performer playing the character of Gerald might demonstrate to the audience that he is ashamed of himself in this extract. You should talk about performance skills, stage directions and use of stage space in your answer.

4) Imagine you're a sound designer working on a production of *An Inspector Calls*. Describe how you would use sound design to add to the overall impact of this extract on the audience.

> Find the part of Act Three where the Inspector gives his final speech. Read from where Mr Birling says "**You must give me a list of those accounts.**" up to where the Inspector exits, then answer Question 5 below.

5) Imagine you're directing a production of *An Inspector Calls*. Explain how a performer playing the character of the Inspector might demonstrate to the audience that he is in control in this extract and elsewhere in the play. You should talk about performance skills, stage directions and use of stage space in your answer.

About the Exam

If you were hoping for a section full of super-useful advice and sample answers, then break out the confetti and celebrate, because that's exactly what this is. Done? Good, now sweep up that confetti and get reading.

'An Inspector Calls' will be assessed in a written exam

1) One section of your exam will require you to answer questions on *An Inspector Calls*. The questions will be about an <u>extract</u> from the play which <u>you'll be given</u> in the exam.

2) You'll be <u>assessed</u> on your <u>knowledge</u> of <u>how</u> the play could be <u>developed</u> and <u>performed</u>.

3) There will be a mixture of <u>shorter and longer questions</u>. Manage your <u>time carefully</u> so you have <u>plenty of time</u> to answer the longer questions — if a question is worth <u>twice the marks</u> of another, you should spend <u>twice as long</u> on it.

You'll answer from different perspectives

1) The questions will ask you to write from the perspectives of a <u>performer</u>, <u>director</u> and <u>designer</u>:

- As a **PERFORMER**, you'll need to think about <u>how</u> and <u>why</u> you would use your performance skills to portray a certain <u>character</u>. This should include <u>physical skills</u> and <u>vocal skills</u>.
- As a **DIRECTOR**, you'll need to consider how you would bring a <u>written text</u> to life <u>on stage</u> by directing actors to use <u>performance skills</u> and using <u>production elements</u> (e.g. costumes, props).
- As a **DESIGNER**, you'll need to describe how you'd use a <u>design element</u> to enhance the impact of a <u>play</u>. This requires a good <u>understanding</u> of areas like <u>set</u>, <u>lighting</u> and <u>sound</u>.

2) You <u>can't</u> just learn about the roles and responsibilities of <u>one type</u> of theatre maker — over the course of the written exam, you'll be expected to answer from <u>all three perspectives</u>.

You'll always need to write about certain aspects

1) No matter which perspective you're writing from, there are some <u>general points</u> you'll need to <u>consider</u>:

- Priestley's <u>intentions</u> and what he wants to convey — <u>stage directions</u> are useful for this.
- How the play's <u>historical</u>, <u>social</u> and <u>theatrical contexts</u> might <u>affect</u> a production.
- The <u>genre</u> and <u>style</u> of the play. You should explore how these can be <u>conveyed</u> to the <u>audience</u>.
- The <u>roles</u> and <u>responsibilities</u> of <u>theatre makers</u> and any <u>challenges</u> they may face.
- The <u>effect</u> of the performance on the <u>audience</u> — this should be <u>central</u> to your answer, <u>whichever</u> perspective you're writing from.

2) To get <u>top marks</u> in the exam, you should <u>also</u>:

- Use accurate <u>technical language</u> when describing <u>performance skills</u> and <u>design features</u>.
- Use <u>examples</u> (e.g. <u>quotes</u> and <u>context</u>) to show <u>understanding</u> of the play and <u>support</u> your points.
- Give <u>specific</u>, <u>detailed</u> suggestions on <u>how</u> you'd <u>perform</u>, <u>design</u> or <u>direct</u> a production to help the examiner <u>visualise</u> your ideas.

About the Exam

Read the extract carefully before you begin

1) All the exam questions about *An Inspector Calls* will ask you to refer to the extract, so make sure you've fully understood it before you start writing.

2) Read each question carefully, then read through the extract. Think about what happens before and after the extract to help you work out how it fits in with the rest of the play. It's important to show an understanding of the play as a whole in your answers.

3) Highlight any important words or phrases (including stage directions). You might also want to annotate the extract as you go along.

4) For shorter answers, you should start writing as soon as you feel comfortable with the extract. But for longer answers, you should plan out a few key ideas for your answers. You could do this by jotting down some bullet points or making a quick diagram (see p. 76).

5) Your answer should be coherent — not just a list of different possibilities for the extract. For example, if you start writing about a naturalistic approach, don't swap to a non-naturalistic one halfway through. A good plan will help to make sure your ideas flow and are well-structured.

Shorter answers should be concise

Remember that you shouldn't spend too much time on short-answer questions that aren't worth many marks. Your answers will need to be snappy and straight to the point. Have a look at this example:

> Find the part of Act Two where the Inspector is questioning Sybil Birling. Read from where the Inspector says "**So she'd come to you for assistance**" up to the end of Act Two, then answer the question below.

Turn to p. 76-79 for examples of what a longer question and answer might look like.

> Imagine you are going to play the Inspector. He asserts "I shall do my duty." in this extract. Give three examples of how you would use performance skills to communicate his sense of purpose to the audience during the extract. Provide a reason for each of your examples.

The first sentence begins with a concise example.

___I would stand during this extract and keep my arms crossed. Standing while the other characters are seated and using closed body language would convey how the Inspector is in control of the situation, and that he has a very clear purpose.

Every suggestion is supported with an appropriate reason.

___When the Inspector *"looks at his watch"*, I would start quietly tapping the seconds out on the table with my fingers until Eric enters. This would give the sense that the Inspector is counting down until Eric's entrance, which would reinforce the Inspector's omniscience and his determination to seek out the truth.

The answer refers to precise moments from the extract.

The answer gives examples of both physical and vocal skills.

___I would deliver my lines using an even, regular pace during this extract to make the Inspector seem calm and focused on his purpose.

Manage your time carefully in the exam...

EXAM TIP

The questions will be worth different marks in the exam. Make sure you don't spend all your time on questions that are worth fewer marks — plan ahead roughly how long you should spend on each one.

Sample Question and Answer

Here's how one of the longer questions in your exam could look. There's a fair bit of detail required, so have a good read through to try to get a sense of how much depth you need to go into in the actual exam.

Here's a sample question about performance

Here's what a long question about <u>performance</u> might look like:

You won't have to hunt for the extract in the exam — it'll be printed in your exam paper.

> Find the part of Act Two where the Inspector is questioning Sybil Birling.
> Read from where the Inspector says **"So she'd come to you for assistance"** up to the end of Act Two, then answer the question below.
>
> Sybil Birling tries to resist the Inspector's questions and moral message throughout the play.
>
> You are directing a production of *An Inspector Calls*. Discuss how the actor playing Sybil could show the audience the character's attitude towards the Inspector in this extract and in the play as a whole. You must refer to the use of voice, physicality, stage directions and stage space.

Here's how you could plan your answer...

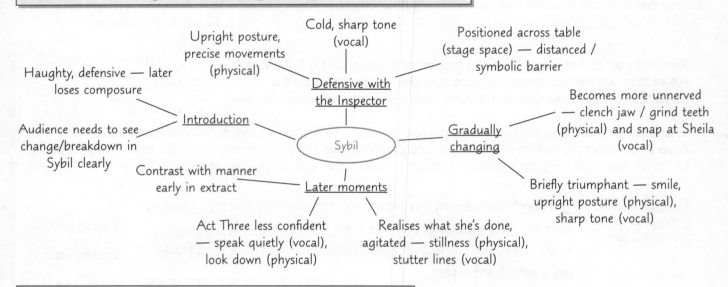

Cold, sharp tone (vocal)

Upright posture, precise movements (physical)

Positioned across table (stage space) — distanced / symbolic barrier

Haughty, defensive — later loses composure

<u>Defensive with the Inspector</u>

Becomes more unnerved — clench jaw / grind teeth (physical) and snap at Sheila (vocal)

<u>Introduction</u>

Sybil

<u>Gradually changing</u>

Audience needs to see change/breakdown in Sybil clearly

Contrast with manner early in extract

<u>Later moments</u>

Briefly triumphant — smile, upright posture (physical), sharp tone (vocal)

Act Three less confident — speak quietly (vocal), look down (physical)

Realises what she's done, agitated — stillness (physical), stutter lines (vocal)

... and here's how you could write it

At the start of the extract, Sybil is cold, abrupt and defiant. She is offended by the Inspector's questions, and refuses to accept his message that her family is responsible for Eva/Daisy's death. To reflect this, I would direct an actor playing Sybil to be haughty and defensive towards the Inspector. At the very end of the extract, Sybil is shocked and distressed when it is revealed that Eric was the father of Eva/Daisy's unborn child. This loss of composure allows the Inspector to take control of the situation. At the end of the extract, I would direct an actor playing Sybil to clearly show her distress using performance skills and proxemics to emphasise the emotional impact of this extract, as well as effectively conveying Sybil's fear that the Inspector will make her family's scandal public.

> Keep your introduction <u>brief</u> and <u>focused</u> on the <u>question</u>.

Sample Question and Answer

This <u>explains</u> the overall <u>effect</u> which is being <u>communicated</u>.

At the start of the extract, I would direct an actor playing Sybil to use physical and vocal skills to show that she is annoyed by the Inspector's questions, but she is not intimidated by him. Earlier in Act Two, Sybil attempts to assert herself over the Inspector by entering the stage *"briskly and self-confidently"*. I would direct an actor to maintain this self-assurance at the start of the extract by using an upright posture and precise movements (for example, carefully adjusting her clothes or hair). I would also direct an actor to use an exaggeratedly cold and sharp tone of voice with the Inspector to show Sybil's annoyance. Using closed body language (for instance, her hands could rest on the table, face down and crossed on top of each other) would also help to show that Sybil is irritated by the Inspector's questions. I would position the two actors on opposite sides of the Birlings' dining table to suggest that Sybil is trying to separate herself from the Inspector. This use of stage space would create distance between the actors, communicating to the audience that the pair have an uneasy relationship, as well as symbolising that Sybil refuses to see things from the Inspector's perspective.

This shows <u>good awareness</u> of the play <u>as a whole</u>.

Always explain the <u>effect</u> of your performance <u>decisions</u>.

Don't forget to include examples of <u>stage space</u>.

Later in the extract, Sybil becomes unnerved as the Inspector presses her about her treatment of Eva/Daisy. I would direct an actor playing Sybil to use her physical performance to make this change clear, for example by clenching her jaw or grinding her teeth. An actor playing Sybil could also snap at Sheila when she says *"Be quiet, Sheila!"*. Increasing the volume, pitch and pace of her speech would give the impression that Sybil is becoming increasingly unnerved by the Inspector.

Explain how the performance <u>develops</u> during the extract.

Sybil briefly regains her confidence when the Inspector agrees with her that the man who got Eva/Daisy pregnant should be held responsible. The stage directions say that she *"triumphantly"* delivers the line *"I'm glad to hear it"* to the Inspector. To reflect this, I would direct an actor playing Sybil to smile smugly, make her posture upright again and return to a sharp tone of voice with the Inspector, to show that her confidence and composure have returned, suggesting that she no longer feels threatened by the Inspector.

Use <u>short quotes</u> to make it clear to the examiner <u>which part</u> of the extract you're referring to.

This considers the <u>impact</u> of the portrayal on the <u>audience</u>.

This triumphant attitude towards the Inspector would make Sybil's sudden loss of composure at the end of the extract more shocking for the audience. When Sybil realises that the Inspector's questions have led her to accidently accuse Eric, she becomes *"agitated"* again. I would direct an actor playing Sybil to suddenly freeze at this point and choke and stutter over her lines to show that she is too shocked to move or to speak properly. An actor could also slump into a chair when she delivers the line *"But surely... I mean..."*. This would suggest that she is so distraught that she is too weak to stand, and that she is terrified of the Inspector making the scandal public. An actor playing Sybil could build upon this shock and distress in Act Three, by delivering her lines more quietly and casting her eyes downwards to show how she has been broken by the Inspector.

Make sure you give <u>reasons</u> for <u>why</u> you'd use a particular performance skill.

Finish your answer with a <u>short conclusion</u>.

These changes in physical and vocal performance would show how Sybil's attitude towards the Inspector changes when she realises that he is in full control of the situation, as she is terrified at the power he has over her family's reputation.

At least you don't have the Inspector as your examiner...

With a longer answer like this, you need to write quite a lot to make sure you've gone into enough depth, but that also means you have to be careful not to fill your writing with waffle — the key is a focused plan.

Sample Question and Answer

It's your lucky day — here's another long sample answer, but just to spice things up a bit, this one's from the perspective of a designer. Once again, your answer should include a lot of detail, so planning is key...

Here's a sample question about design

Here's what a long question about <u>design</u> might look like:

> Find the part of Act Two where the Inspector is questioning Sybil Birling.
> Read from where the Inspector says "**So she'd come to you for assistance**"
> up to the end of Act Two, then answer the question below.
>
> As a designer, discuss how you would use **either** lighting **or** sound **or** set design during this extract to contribute to the impact of the production on the audience.

Here's how you could plan your answer...

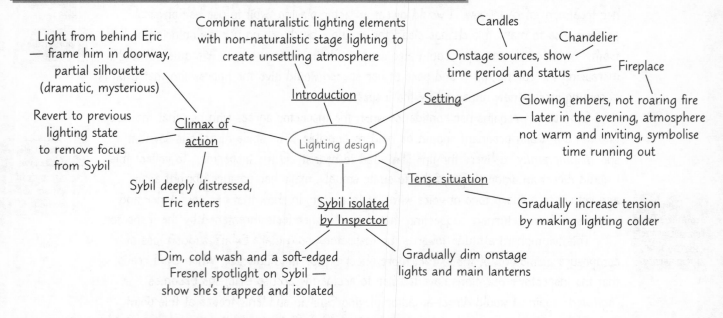

... and here's how you could write it

This describes the <u>overall effect</u> you want to achieve.

As a lighting designer for this extract, I would combine naturalistic and non-naturalistic stage lighting to show the setting and contribute to the unsettling atmosphere on stage. This would reinforce the tension for the audience before the abrupt cliffhanger at the end of the act.

I would use naturalistic onstage lighting sources to help communicate the setting, time of day and the Birlings' wealth and status. A fire positioned upstage centre would help to show that it is evening, as would candles on the table, while a chandelier hung from above the stage would show the Birlings' wealth. Given safety considerations, it would be impractical to use open flames on stage, so the chandelier, the candles

Concise point, followed by appropriate <u>justification</u> for the design idea.

Sample Question and Answer

and fire could be electric, which would also make it easier to control them remotely. Rather than having a roaring fire, I would use fairy lights on a flickering setting to represent smouldering embers, because this would be less distracting than a flame effect. Furthermore, a smouldering fire would make the Birlings' dining room seem less warm, bright and inviting. Embers could also be subtly symbolic and fit in with the themes of the play — a dying fire would reflect that time is running out for the Birling family, and for society in general, if the Inspector's message is not heeded.

> **Considers how design contributes to overall meaning of the play.**

I would start the extract with *"pink and intimate"* lighting that would have been in place since Mrs Birling first entered in Act Two; this would be the same lighting as at the start of the play to show that Mrs Birling is oblivious to what is going on. This warmer lighting would then allow me to gradually make it seem colder and harsher during the extract while Mrs Birling is being questioned. This would show that the Inspector is asserting his control over her with his questions. Changing the lighting to be colder and harsher over the course of the scene would also help to emphasise to the audience the increase in tension, right up until the climactic end when Eric enters. As the Inspector continues to question Sybil, I would gradually dim the light from the onstage light sources like the fire and the chandelier, and switch to a more non-naturalistic style of lighting by using a floodlight and a blue gel to create a dim, cold wash of light on stage. I would combine this with a soft-edged, white Fresnel spotlight focused on Sybil. The spotlight would communicate to the audience that Sybil is isolated and trapped by the Inspector and his questions. It would also suggest how single-minded the Inspector is — while he is questioning Sybil, he is focused solely on her.

> **Shows knowledge of the play as a whole and how the extract best fits into it.**

> **Confidently uses detailed technical language.**

I would place a lantern behind the doorway where Eric enters so that he is lit from behind with a white light, somewhat obscuring him from the audience to create a partial silhouette, while removing the Fresnel spotlight from Sybil. This would draw the audience's attention to him, and away from Sybil. Partially obscuring his features with shadow would also make him seem suspicious and mysterious to the audience and reflect the fact that he has been secretive with his family. Once Eric has entered, I would dim the backlight behind him so that he can be seen clearly by the audience. This would also reflect the way that his identity was gradually revealed to Sybil by the Inspector. At this point I would use a floodlight to make the light on stage brighter and more even. I would also increase the intensity of the onstage lighting sources (the fire, candles and chandelier) to make the lighting seem more naturalistic again. This would allow the audience to see how the characters react to Eric. Their *"inquiring stares"* would help the audience understand the importance of the moment by giving a sense of finality to the extract and to the act.

> **Effect on the audience's understanding of the play is central to the answer.**

> **A wide range of different effects described and explained.**

> **Quote from play used to explain precisely when the effect will be used.**

Design your answer as carefully as you'd design a set...

... you don't want any of your arguments falling down and hitting the examiner on the head. Your answer should be coherent, not just cobbled together, so read the question and extract carefully before you start.

Glossary

apron	A part of a stage that extends beyond the curtain.
backlighting	When the stage is lit from behind to produce silhouettes of the actors.
backstory	The events that have happened to a character before the action of the play.
blackout	When the stage lights are turned off between scenes or at the end of a performance.
blocking	The process of positioning the actors on stage and planning their movements to maintain good sightlines for the audience.
body language	The way movements, posture and gestures can show how someone feels without speaking.
Brecht, Bertolt	A German theatre maker who played a major role in the development of Epic Theatre.
catharsis	The sense of release felt by an audience when a play makes them feel strong emotions.
cliffhanger	When a conflict isn't fully resolved, leaving the audience wondering what happens next.
climax	The turning point in a play, where tension is at its highest. When the tension is resolved again straight away, this can create an anticlimax.
crime thriller	A genre where the plot revolves around a crime and the question of 'whodunnit?'.
cyclorama	A curved screen at the back of the stage which can have scenery projected onto it.
dialogue	The general term for any lines spoken between characters.
diction	The quality (or clarity) of a performer's vocal expression.
diegetic sound	A sound that can be heard by the characters in a play.
downlighting	When the stage is lit from above to highlight certain characters or cast shadows.
dramatic irony	When the audience knows something that the characters don't.
end-on stage	A proscenium arch stage without the arch to frame it.
Epic Theatre	A style of theatre made famous by Bertolt Brecht. It tries to distance the audience from the action of the play so that they can concentrate on the overall message.
flat	A wooden frame with canvas stretched over it which is painted and used as scenery.
floodlight	A type of stage lantern which casts a broad wash of light onto the stage.
fourth wall	The imaginary barrier that separates the audience from the world of the play on stage.
Fresnel spotlight	A type of stage lantern which casts a beam with a softly defined edge.
gel	A piece of coloured, heat-resistant, plastic film used to change the colour of a lantern's beam.
genre	The type of story a play is telling (e.g. comedy, tragedy).
gesture	A movement made by part of the body (e.g. arms, head) to convey a character's emotions.
gobo	A thin, metal disc with shapes cut into it which can be slotted into a lantern to project patterns or images onto the stage or a backdrop.
incidental music	Any music which accompanies a performance and is used to create mood or tension.
inflection	Changes in the pitch and tone of a person's voice as they speak.
intonation	The rise and fall of a performer's voice to create a natural pattern of speech.
mood	The atmosphere at a particular moment that creates a feeling or emotion for the audience.

Glossary

morality play	A genre of religious play from the Middle Ages, performed to warn against the dangers of sin.
naturalism	A style of theatre which tries to recreate real life on stage as closely as possible. In contrast, a non-naturalistic style includes features that remind the audience what they're watching isn't real.
non-diegetic sound	A sound that can't be heard by the characters in the play.
phrasing	The way a character's dialogue is broken up into sections when spoken by an actor.
physicality	How an actor uses their body (e.g. posture, gestures, movement) in a performance.
pitch	How high or low an actor's voice is.
posture	The position a character holds themselves in when sitting or standing.
profile spotlight	A type of stage lantern that produces a sharply defined beam. These lanterns are used to focus on a particular character or part of the stage.
prop	An item on stage that the characters can interact with.
proscenium arch stage	A box-shaped stage which is set back from the audience so that only the front end is open to them, framed by the proscenium arch itself.
proxemics	The use of the physical space between the actors on stage to create meaning.
Received Pronunciation	An accent that is considered the accent of Standard English in the UK and has the highest social status.
rostrum	A raised platform which is used to introduce different levels to the stage (plural rostra).
silhouette	A dark outline of the performers or scenery which is created using a backlight.
site-specific theatre	A style of staging which temporarily transforms somewhere that isn't a theatre into a performance space. This space often resembles the play's setting in some way.
Socialism	A set of political beliefs based on the idea of sharing wealth and power more equally.
soundscape	A collection of individual sounds that are layered up to create a strong sense of place.
stage directions	Any instructions written in a script by the playwright to explain how a play should be performed.
stage furniture	Any moveable object on stage which isn't a costume, a prop or a part of the scenery.
stereotype	An oversimplified idea about what a person is like, based on a group they belong to.
strobe	A type of stage lantern which rapidly flashes on and off.
structure	The shape of a play's narrative, including the order in which it's shown to the audience.
style	The way in which a director chooses to interpret a performance text on stage.
subtext	The underlying or hidden meaning behind a character's speech and actions.
symbolism	The use of props, gestures, setting, lighting, etc. to represent other things and create meaning.
theatre in the round	A style of staging which seats the audience on all sides of a central stage.
thrust stage	A stage which extends out into the audience, so that they're standing or sitting on three sides.
traverse stage	A long, narrow stage which runs between the audience, who face the stage on both sides.
underscoring	Incidental music that is played quietly during a scene under spoken dialogue or visual action.
uplighting	When the stage is lit from below to create an unusual or unsettling effect.
well-made play	A genre characterised by suspense, many revelations and a neat resolution.

Index

The Characters in 'An Inspector Calls'

Phew! After all that drama, I reckon you deserve a bit of a break. So grab a cup of tea and your favourite kind of biscuit, make yourself comfortable and enjoy *An Inspector Calls — The Cartoon...*

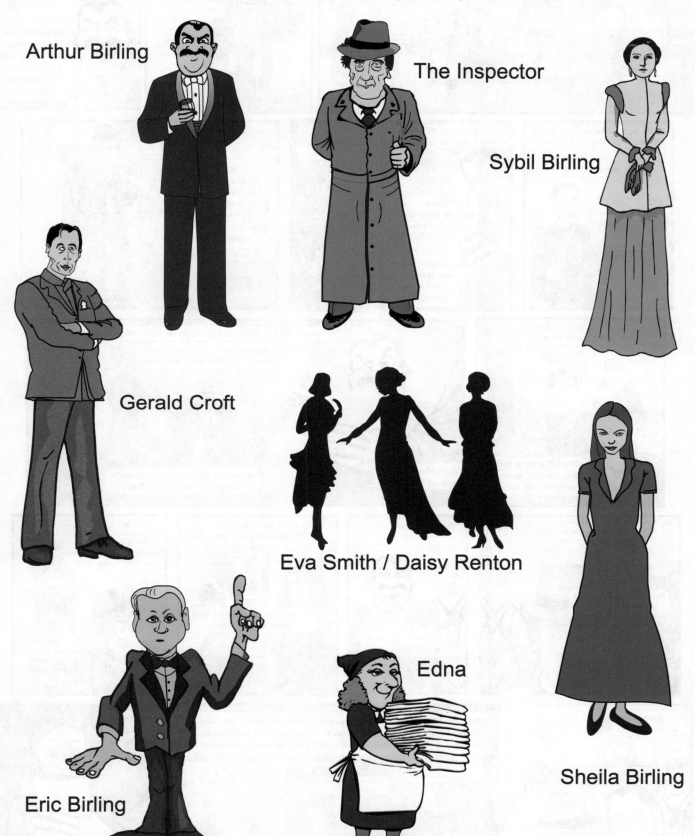

Arthur Birling

The Inspector

Sybil Birling

Gerald Croft

Eva Smith / Daisy Renton

Eric Birling

Edna

Sheila Birling

J. B. Priestley's 'An Inspector Calls'

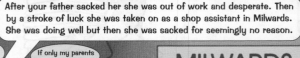